SPLENDID DESSERTS

Deliciously Sweet & Low-Cal
SUGARLESS DESSERTS
Nutritional Analysis Included

❖ **DEDICATION** ❖

I am thankful to God who was the source of my inspiration, and to my husband, Ian, and sons, Daniel and Jonathan, for their constant loving support and encouragement, as well as to our extended family and friends.

by Jennifer Eloff

 **all recipes use SPLENDA® Granular**

Front Cover
Frosted Strawberry Cheesecake, page 40

Splendid Desserts, Revised Edition
by
Jennifer Eloff

First Printing – September 1993
Second Printing – September 1994

Copyright © 1993 by
Eureka Publishing
P.O. Box 2305
Station "M"
Calgary, Alberta
Canada, T2P 2M6

Canadian Cataloguing in Publication Data

Eloff, Jennifer , 1957-

  Splendid desserts

  Includes index.
  ISBN 1-895292-30-1

1. Desserts.   2. Sugar-free diet – Recipes.
3. Low-calorie diet – Recipes.   I. Title.

TX773.E46 1993   641.8'6   C93-098171-5

Dishes and Accessories courtesy of:
Eaton's, Calgary, Alberta
Primrose, Calgary, Alberta

Photography by:
Ross Hutchinson
Hutchinson & Company
Calgary, Alberta

Designed, Printed and Produced in Canada by:
Centax Books, a Division of PrintWest Ltd.
Publishing Director, Photo Designer & Food Stylist: Margo Embury
1150 Eighth Avenue, Regina, Saskatchewan, Canada S4R 1C9
(306) 525-2304   FAX (306) 757-2439

❖ TABLE OF CONTENTS ❖

Recipes have been tested in U.S. Standard measurements. Common metric measurements are given as a convenience for those who are more familiar with metric. Recipes have not been tested in metric.

NOTE TO DIABETICS: Since sucralose, SPLENDA® LOW-CALORIE SWEETENER, is chemically inert, it will not provide the emergency benefits of sugar for a hypoglycemic reaction. Sucralose does not break down during its passage through the body.

The nutritional analyses of these recipes were calculated using the Health and Diet Pro Computer program. These analyses have been calculated as accurately as possible, but should only be used as a guideline. Optional ingredients are factored in only when indicated.

RECIPE	Page	Serv	Serv size	Carbo	Protein	Fat	Fiber	Sodium	Cal
BEVERAGES				grams	grams	grams	grams	mg	
Hot Spiced Apple Drink	8	4	1 cup	32.1	0.0	0.0	0.3	7.0	128
Lemonade Concentrate	8	6	¼ cup	5.1	0.1	0.1	0.0	6.4	19
Fruit Cocktail Concentrate	8	9	¼ cup	10.4	0.3	0.1	0.0	4.9	41
Spiced Apple Yogurt Shake	9	3	1 cup	21.1	7.0	0.0	0.5	101.7	113
Strawberry Banana Yogurt Shake	9	4	1 cup	22.9	5.8	0.6	0.5	75.6	118
Chocolate Banana Yogurt Shake	9	4	1 cup	23.9	5.8	0.6	0.3	75.6	121
Strawberry Yogurt Shake	9	4	1 cup	14.0	5.6	0.4	0.7	75.4	82
Peach Yogurt Shake	9	4	1 cup	17.5	5.6	0.0	0.4	75.0	93
BREADS - CRÊPES, PANCAKES, SCONES, MUFFINS & LOAVES									
Swedish Crêpes	10	20	1 crêpe	11.1	3.3	2.4	0.0	67.1	80
Yogurt Cheese – a generous filling for crêpes	10	8	¼ cup	4.3	3.3	0.0	0.0	43.5	31
Swedish Waffles	11	16	1 waffle	13.1	3.1	2.4	0.0	120.3	87
Swedish Pancakes	11	15	1 pancake	14.0	3.3	2.5	0.0	128.3	93
Blueberry Pancakes	11	15	1 pancake	16.7	3.5	2.7	0.3	129.5	104
Scones	12	12	1 scone	16.8	3.0	5.8	0.1	191.8	132
Pineapple Raspberry Muffins	12	12	1 muffin	19.7	3.8	5.9	0.5	134.3	148
Large Blueberry Muffins	13	18	1 muffin	19.8	3.7	4.0	0.3	113.0	131
Large Blueberry Muffins	13	12	1 muffin	29.7	5.5	6.0	0.4	169.5	196
Apple Cinnamon Streusel Muffins	14	18	1 muffin	14.0	2.6	6.3	0.1	151.7	125
Banana Oatmeal Muffins	15	18	1 muffin	23.3	3.5	3.1	0.7	214.5	132
Chocolate Cheesecake Muffins	16	18	1 muffin	23.0	5.2	12.3	0.1	252.5	222
Apple Cinnamon Swirl Loaf	19	16	1 slice	15.4	2.8	4.8	0.1	136.3	117
Applesauce Nut Bread	20	16	1 slice	16.1	2.8	6.7	0.2	95.3	135
Banana Loaf – 2 large loaves	20	32	1 slice	18.3	2.6	4.6	0.2	131.2	124
Cranberry Orange Loaf	21	16	1 slice	16.8	2.1	3.3	0.1	116.0	106
Easy Cinnamon-Swirl Yeast Loaf	22	16	1 slice	22.6	4.1	7.8	0.2	124.4	177
CAKES – COFFEECAKES & CAKES									
Zucchini Almond Coffeecake with Almond Cream Cheese Icing	23	24	1 serving	3.7	1.7	4.5	0.0	114.0	61
Strawberry Streusel Coffeecake – serving size smaller	24	12	1 serving	26.0	4.2	12.4	0.6	186.8	232
Blueberry Streusel Coffeecake	25	24	1 serving	12.0	1.8	4.9	0.2	115.0	99
Apple Cinnamon Coffeecake	26	24	1 serving	16.3	2.4	4.4	0.3	157.2	115
White Cake with condensed milk & without frosting	27	12	1 serving	26.1	5.3	9.8	0.1	413.1	216
Marble Cake with condensed milk & without frosting	27	12	1 serving	26.8	5.4	10.0	0.1	414.4	219
Orange Mandarin Cake with orange frosting	28	12	1 serving	30.7	9.1	11.7	0.2	541.6	267
Black Forest Cake with commercial low-calorie dessert topping	29	12	1 serving	17.8	3.1	8.5	0.1	76.8	157
Black Forest Cake with heavy whipping cream	29	12	1 serving	18.1	3.8	22.2	0.1	91.6	282
Chocolate Cake without frosting	30	12	1 serving	25.5	3.8	10.0	0.1	365.4	206
Carrot Cake (brownie style) with cream cheese icing	31	18	1 serving	15.0	3.5	5.4	0.1	144.1	123
Carrot Cake with cream cheese icing	31	9	1 serving	30.1	6.9	10.9	0.3	288.2	246
Banana Chiffon Cake with chocolate nut sauce	32	12	1 serving	28.7	5.3	11.2	0.2	404.6	235
CRUSTS FOR CHEESECAKES AND PIES									
Almond Crumb Crust	33	12	1 serving	8.7	1.5	6.1	1.0	88.0	91
Almond Crumb Crust	33	8	1 serving	13.0	2.2	9.2	1.2	131.9	136
Almond Crumb Crust, reduced fat & ¼ cup ground almonds	33	12	1 serving	8.6	1.3	3.0	0.8	74.1	65
Almond Crumb Crust, reduced fat & ¼ cup ground almonds	33	8	1 serving	12.9	2.0	4.5	1.2	111.2	97
Crumb Crust with graham crumbs	37	12	1 serving	10.0	1.1	2.2	0.9	88.9	63
Crumb Crust with graham crumbs	37	8	1 serving	15.0	1.6	3.3	1.4	133.3	94
Crumb Crust with ½ graham crumbs & ½ grape-nuts cereal	37	12	1 serving	14.0	1.8	2.0	1.6	105.5	76
Crumb Crust with ½ graham crumbs & ½ grape-nuts cereal	37	8	1 serving	21.0	2.6	3.0	2.3	158.3	114
Sugarless Sweet Dough Crust	45	12	1 serving	8.0	1.5	2.8	0.0	59.2	65
Sugarless Sweet Dough Crust	45	8	1 serving	12.1	2.3	4.3	0.0	88.7	98
Sugarless Chocolate Sweet Dough Crust	45	12	1 serving	7.5	1.3	3.2	0.0	59.1	63
Sugarless Chocolate Sweet Dough Crust	45	8	1 serving	11.2	1.9	4.7	0.0	88.7	94
Vanilla Wafer Crust	40	12	1 serving	9.9	0.7	4.3	0.0	68.3	79
Vanilla Wafer Crust	40	8	1 serving	14.9	1.0	6.5	0.0	102.5	119
Vanilla Wafer Crust with reduced fat (see helpful hints)	40	12	1 serving	10.1	0.9	3.3	0.0	63.9	73
Vanilla Wafer Crust with reduced fat (see helpful hints)	40	8	1 serving	15.1	1.4	4.9	0.0	95.8	109
Chocolate Crumb Crust	41	12	1 serving	10.2	0.9	4.4	0.9	102.5	79
Chocolate Crumb Crust	41	8	1 serving	15.2	1.3	6.6	1.4	153.8	119
Chocolate Crumb Crust with reduced fat (see helpful hints)	41	12	1 serving	10.4	1.1	2.3	0.9	88.9	65
Chocolate Crumb Crust with reduced fat (see helpful hints)	41	8	1 serving	15.7	1.7	3.5	1.4	133.4	98
Single Crust for Pies	45	8	1 serving	8.9	1.2	4.9	0.0	26.2	85
Double Crust	55	10	1 serving	19.9	2.7	12.2	0.1	53.8	202
Cookie Crust – a double crust for the lattice pies	59	10	1 serving	18.9	3.0	13.4	0.1	10.5	209
WHIPPED TOPPINGS									
Commercial Low-Calorie Dessert Topping – 2 cups	7	12	1 serving	0.9	0.1	0.9	0.0	0.0	12
Commercial Low-Calorie Dessert Topping – 2 cups	7	8	¼ cup	1.4	0.2	1.4	0.0	0.0	18
Sugarless Whipped Topping – 2 cups	11	12	1 serving	1.8	1.0	1.5	0.0	15.6	26
Sugarless Whipped Topping – 2 cups	11	8	¼ cup	2.7	1.5	2.2	0.0	23.4	38
CHEESECAKES - FILLINGS ONLY, UNLESS OTHERWISE NOTED									
Lemon Almond Cheesecake with a sprinkle of 1 tbsp. almonds	33	12	1 serving	8.5	9.4	8.1	0.0	219.3	143
Orange Mandarin Cheesecake	34	12	1 serving	8.5	9.3	7.7	0.0	219.3	141
Lime Cheesecake	34	12	1 serving	8.4	9.3	7.7	0.0	219.3	139
Raspberry Lemon Cheesecake with Raspberry Topping	37	12	1 serving	16.7	10.0	8.6	1.0	212.1	183

RECIPE	Page	Serv	Serv size	Carbo	Protein	Fat	Fiber	Sodium	Cal
				grams	grams	grams	grams	mg	
CHEESECAKES - (Continued)									
Blueberry Swirl Cheesecake – no topping required	38	12	1 serving	14.6	10.0	8.6	0.3	212.6	174
Strawberry Cheesecake with Strawberry Topping	39	12	1 serving	13.0	9.4	8.3	0.5	218.2	162
Peach Cheesecake with Peach Topping	39	12	1 serving	15.4	9.5	7.7	0.3	219.2	168
Blueberry Cheesecake with Blueberry Topping	39	12	1 serving	15.6	9.5	8.0	0.6	221.4	169
Frosted Strawberry Cheesecake with 2 cups low-cal topping	40	12	1 serving	12.8	9.4	8.3	0.3	184.0	162
Chocolate Swirl Cheesecake – no topping required	41	12	1 serving	7.8	7.0	5.7	0.0	171.9	110
Marbled Black Forest Cheesecake with topping	42	12	1 serving	15.7	9.7	10.4	0.0	192.8	192
Dark Black Forest Cheesecake with topping	44	12	1 serving	17.0	10.5	13.5	0.7	194.9	222
PIES - FILLINGS ONLY, UNLESS OTHERWISE NOTED									
Vanilla Cream Pie	46	8	1 serving	8.6	4.3	3.8	0.0	68.6	86
Banana Cream Pie	47	8	1 serving	17.7	4.6	4.2	0.2	69.4	124
Lemon Cream Pie	47	8	1 serving	8.8	3.8	3.8	0.0	62.2	85
Chocolate Cream Pie	48	8	1 serving	14.1	4.0	4.9	0.3	55.3	110
Milk Tart with crust	49	8	1 serving	12.4	6.0	7.3	0.0	212.2	141
Custard Pie with crust and using egg whites	50	8	1 serving	23.9	4.9	6.9	0.1	130.9	180
Custard Pie with crust and using sugarless whipped topping	50	8	1 serving	26.6	5.6	9.2	0.1	141.8	215
Glazed Blueberry Cheese Pie with Blueberry Topping	51	8	1 serving	15.5	5.8	3.2	0.8	198.5	110
Glazed Strawberry Cheese Pie with Strawberry Topping	51	8	1 serving	11.7	5.8	3.2	0.7	195.5	97
Pineapple Cheese Pie	52	8	1 serving	17.0	7.7	6.6	0.2	169.1	156
Peach Cheese Pie	52	8	1 serving	15.7	7.8	6.6	0.3	168.4	152
Strawberry Rhubarb Pie, double crust, serving size smaller	55	10	1 serving	45.2	2.8	12.9	0.7	61.4	302
Strawberry Pie	56	8	1 serving	9.1	0.5	0.5	1.0	11.2	39
Blueberry Pie	56	8	1 serving	14.1	0.5	0.5	1.1	15.2	57
Bumbleberry Tart – no topping required	57	8	1 serving	17.6	1.1	0.8	2.7	14.1	74
Blueberry/Strawberry Flan with sponge cake and topping	58	8	1 serving	28.1	6.1	9.8	1.1	229.6	223
Apple Lattice Pie with cookie crust – serving size smaller	59	10	1 serving	33.3	3.1	14.0	0.5	17.3	274
Peach Lattice Pie – serving size smaller	60	10	1 serving	15.8	0.6	0.0	0.6	0.0	63
Cherry Lattice Pie – serving size smaller	60	10	1 serving	15.7	0.9	0.9	0.2	8.3	69
Fruit Pizza with crust and topping	61	12	1 serving	19.2	6.4	9.9	0.3	246.8	191
PUDDINGS, MOUSSES & ICE CREAMS									
Spiced Date Pudding with lemon sauce	62	6	1 serving	51.9	5.3	4.0	0.8	339.8	255
Snow Pudding with egg whites	63	4	1 cup	5.7	1.6	0.1	0.0	28.2	35
Snow Pudding with sugarless whipped topping	63	4	1 cup	9.1	1.9	2.9	0.0	32.4	75
Orange Jelly	63	4	1 cup	9.4	0.3	0.0	0.1	1.3	49
Banana Citrus Mousse with commercial low-calorie topping	64	4	1 serving	45.0	2.0	2.9	0.9	2.5	207
Banana Citrus Mousse with sugarless whipped topping	64	4	1 serving	46.4	3.3	3.7	0.9	25.9	228
Chocolate Banana Mousse with egg whites and plain yogurt	65	4	1 serving	23.4	3.3	2.0	0.4	38.9	122
Strawberry Banana Mousse with egg whites and plain yogurt	65	4	1 serving	18.3	3.2	1.6	0.7	38.8	101
Chocolate Strawberry Cream Cups	66	10	1 cup	16.4	2.3	13.1	1.9	24.0	170
Chocolate Cocoa Cream Cups	67	10	1 cup	15.0	2.1	13.1	1.5	23.8	164
Chocolate Orange Cream Cups	67	10	1 cup	14.9	2.2	12.9	1.5	23.8	163
Vanilla Ice Cream	68	32	½ cup	5.7	2.9	3.5	0.0	55.6	64
Banana Ice Cream	68	32	½ cup	10.5	3.1	3.7	0.1	55.8	85
Peach Ice Cream	68	32	½ cup	8.6	3.0	3.5	0.2	55.6	76
Strawberry Ice Cream	68	32	½ cup	7.2	3.0	3.6	0.3	55.8	71
Chocolate Ice Cream	68	16	½ cup	6.6	2.6	8.1	0.2	55.8	106
Summer Fruit Sorbets	69	2	1 serving	11.6	0.8	0.8	1.4	0.8	50
Frozen Strawberry Yogurt	70	32	½ cup	7.6	3.9	1.0	0.2	53.3	55
Frozen Blueberry Yogurt	70	32	½ cup	7.6	2.3	1.2	0.3	30.7	49
COOKIES									
Oatmeal Raisin Cookies	73	20	1 cookie	12.0	2.1	5.3	0.5	63.7	102
Coconut Cookies	73	25	1 cookie	6.6	1.0	4.2	0.1	60.3	66
Jumbo Spice Cookies	74	18	1 cookie	11.9	2.2	5.3	0.0	89.6	102
Twin Coconut Drops	74	20	1 cookie	5.0	1.3	5.0	0.6	20.1	67
SQUARES									
Banana Chocolate Oat Squares with chocolate	75	9	1 square	28.1	4.1	6.3	2.3	53.4	176
Cream Cheese Swirl Brownies	76	16	1 brownie	7.1	2.2	4.0	0.0	82.6	71
Pineapple Coconut Squares	77	24	1 square	11.0	1.3	5.3	0.3	48.5	95
Lemon Delight Squares	78	16	1 square	11.4	2.5	3.7	0.5	71.3	89
ICINGS									
Pudding Icing	79	12	1 serving	6.6	1.2	1.5	0.0	15.8	45
Chocolate Cream Frosting	79	12	1 serving	6.3	1.2	2.2	0.0	14.1	47
Mocha Cream Frosting	80	12	1 serving	5.1	0.9	1.9	0.0	10.5	40
Orange Frosting	80	12	1 serving	11.5	0.7	1.1	0.0	2.2	58
SAUCES & JAMS									
Wonderful Creamy Custard Sauce	81	12	¼ cup	5.2	2.3	1.0	0.0	28.8	40
Strawberry Sauce	82	8	¼ cup	3.9	0.3	0.3	0.5	0.3	17
Strawberry Apple Sauce	82	8	¼ cup	4.8	0.3	0.3	0.5	0.5	20
Raspberry Sauce	82	8	¼ cup	4.9	0.3	0.3	1.2	0.0	21
Peach Sauce	82	8	¼ cup	6.1	0.3	0.0	0.3	0.0	24
Blueberry Sauce	83	8	¼ cup	9.2	0.4	0.3	0.6	2.4	38
Applesauce	83	12	¼ cup	13.9	0.0	0.0	0.8	0.0	53
Strawberry Jam	84	67	1 tbsp.	1.8	0.1	0.1	0.2	0.4	8
Peach Jam	84	67	1 tbsp.	2.6	0.1	0.0	0.1	0.3	11
Apricot Jam	84	67	1 tbsp.	2.5	0.2	0.1	0.2	0.4	11
Plum Jam	84	67	1 tbsp.	2.9	0.1	0.1	0.1	0.4	12
Cherry Jam	84	67	1 tbsp.	2.6	0.1	0.1	0.0	0.7	11
Raspberry Jam	84	67	1 tbsp.	2.2	0.1	0.1	0.4	0.3	10
Blueberry Jam	84	67	1 tbsp.	2.7	0.1	0.1	0.2	1.1	11

❖ HELPFUL HINTS ❖

1. *Nutritional Analysis:* This is a new feature for the revised edition of *Splendid Desserts*. For maximum flexibility, crusts, fillings and toppings have been evaluated separately, unless otherwise stated. Simply choose those preferred (mix and match as desired) and add the values for all the categories together for the total nutritional analysis per serving of the dessert. Analyses are calculated for the smaller serving sizes suggested in the recipes. The serving size for the double crust pies has been slightly reduced as indicated in the table. Optional ingredients are factored in only when indicated.

2. *Calories:* Simply by substituting SPLENDA® Granular in a traditional dessert requiring 2 cups (500 mL) of sugar, 1,400 calories are removed! (Sugar: 1 tsp. [5 mL] = 16 cal.; 1 cup [250 mL] = 800 cal. SPLENDA® Granular: 1 tsp. (5 mL) = 2 cal.; 1 cup (250 mL) = 100 cal.) Low-fat, low-calorie ingredients further reduce calories in these recipes. Substitution with regular ingredients will work, but the calories will be higher. Refer to page 43 for a revealing comparison of a regular cheesecake versus a sugar-less, low-fat version!

3. *Reducing Fat:* Egg substitute may be tried instead of large whole eggs in the baked goods. Otherwise, if preferred, use 1 whole egg and for every extra egg required, use 1 egg white plus 1 tsp. (5 mL) water. One large yolk can have as much as 6 grams of fat! Nonstick cooking spray may be used to grease pans. For cheesecakes and pies, choose crusts and toppings carefully in order to add the least number of fat grams per serving. Refer to page 37 for a great low-fat crumb crust. To reduce the fat in the almond, chocolate and vanilla crumb crusts, replace the diet margarine with 1 tbsp. (15 mL) butter, 1 egg white and 1 or more tablespoons (15 mL plus) apple juice or water (see table, page 4). Otherwise, spray the pan with nonstick cooking spray and sprinkle with ⅓ cup (75 mL) crumbs. Instead of partly skimmed ricotta cheese, use the lowest fat cottage cheese available. Use nonfat yogurt in place of light sour cream. Reduce the nuts in baked goods and crusts by ½. Toast the nuts used to intensify their flavor. Reduce the margarine in streusel toppings by ½. When the fat grams are below 0.05, it registers as zero in the analysis.

4. *Preserving desserts and jams:* Many of the baked desserts freeze well. Since sugar normally helps preserve baked goods and jams, refrigeration is preferable. Jams last unopened in the refrigerator for over a year. Opened jam will last several weeks in the refrigerator.

5. Cakes: Perhaps the biggest challenge was in this area. A correct balance of ingredients, as well as the correct technique is required to achieve excellent results. For light-textured cakes, use self-raising cake flour. Unsweetened fruit juice helps the rising process, otherwise you could end up with pancakes! Sweetened condensed milk (1 tbsp. [15 mL]) is used in the white cake recipe to help the rising process.

6. Self-raising cake and pastry flour: To convert ordinary cake and pastry flour to self-raising, use this recipe for equally good results: 1 cup (250 mL) cake flour, 1½ tsp. (7 mL) baking powder, ⅓ tsp. (1.5 mL) salt. Therefore, when using 2½ cups (625 mL) cake flour in the cake recipes, use 3¾ tsp. (19 mL) baking powder and ¾ tsp. (4 mL) salt to convert it to self-raising. Sift all the dry ingredients together, as well as the baking powder and baking soda amounts specified in the recipe.

7. Cheesecakes: These come highly recommended. Calories and fat are greatly reduced compared to regular cheesecakes (see page 43) without compromising taste. Remember cheesecakes taste much better when matured in the refrigerator at least 1 day, preferably more.

8. Pies: These also come highly recommended. Fruit pies can be frozen unbaked or baked, but the former is preferable as the crust will be more tender and the fruit flavor more true.

Freezing an unbaked pie: Add 1 extra tablespoon (15 mL) thickener to the pie. If it is a closed double crust pie, omit the vents in the top crust. Use freezer wrap.

Baking a frozen unbaked pie: Do not thaw. Cut vents in the top crust and bake in a 350°F (180°C) oven for approximately 20 minutes more than required in the recipe.

Freezing a baked fruit pie: Cool and use freezer wrap.

Baking a frozen baked fruit pie: Thaw for 1 hour; bake at 350°F (180°C) for 30 minutes, reduce heat if overbrowning and cover with foil; bake 15-20 minutes more.

9. Egg Whites: Nowadays many people are afraid to use raw egg whites in desserts because of salmonella. Substitute suggestions are given on page 65.

10. Whipped Topping: Beat 1 tsp. (5 mL) cornstarch into 2 cups (500 mL) commercial low-calorie dessert topping for better holding power.

❖ HOT SPICED APPLE DRINK ❖

This special drink is perfect for a frosty day.

4 cups	unsweetened apple juice	1 L
2	cinnamon sticks	2
6	cloves	6
½ cup	SPLENDA® Granular	125 mL

Combine all the ingredients in a large saucepan. Bring to the boil. Boil 5 minutes, then reduce the heat and allow to simmer with the lid on for a further 5 minutes. Remove the spices. Serve hot. **Serves 4.**

❖ LEMONADE CONCENTRATE ❖

Dilute with water for a cool, refreshing drink.

¾ cup	unsweetened lemon juice	175 mL
¾ cup	SPLENDA® Granular	175 mL
¾ cup	cold water	175 mL

Stir all ingredients together. Pour 3-4 tbsp. (45-60 mL) of the concentrate into a 1 cup (250 mL) glass and fill with cold water. Serve with ice.

Try using soda water instead of water for a nice fizzy lemonade. It may be necessary to increase the amount of concentrate when using soda water. **Yield: 1½ cups (375 mL) concentrate.**

❖ FRUIT COCKTAIL CONCENTRATE ❖

Delicious and packed with vitamins.

¾ cup	unsweetened lemon juice	175 mL
¾ cup	unsweetened pineapple juice	175 mL
¾ cup	fresh orange juice OR orange juice from concentrate	175 mL
1½ cups	SPLENDA® Granular	375 mL

Combine all the ingredients. Pour ice-cold water into a glass. Stir in concentrate to your taste. This recipe doubles and triples easily. **Yield: 2¼ cups (550 mL) concentrate.**

❖ SPICED APPLE YOGURT SHAKE ❖

An unusual and satisfying shake.

1 cup	applesauce, page 83	250 mL
¼ cup	SPLENDA® Granular	60 mL
1 cup	skim milk yogurt	250 mL
1 cup	cold skim milk	250 mL

Follow the applesauce recipe. Combine all the ingredients in a blender and process on high speed until smooth. **Serves 3.**

❖ STRAWBERRY BANANA ❖ YOGURT SHAKE

Adapt this basic shake to your favorite flavors.

½ cup	fresh OR frozen, unsweetened strawberries, almost thawed	125 mL
1 cup	mashed banana	250 mL
½ cup	SPLENDA® Granular	125 mL
1 cup	skim milk yogurt	250 mL
1 cup	cold skim milk	250 mL

Combine all the ingredients in a blender and process until smooth. **Serves 4.**

VARIATIONS: Chocolate Banana Yogurt Shake — Use 1½ cups (375 mL) sliced bananas and add 4 tsp. (20 mL) cocoa to above recipe.

Strawberry Yogurt Shake — Replace fruit in above recipe with 1½ cups (375 mL) fresh or frozen, unsweetened strawberries, almost thawed.

Peach Yogurt Shake — Replace fruit in above recipe with 1½ cups (375 mL) fresh or frozen, unsweetened peaches, almost thawed.

See photograph on page 17.

❖ SWEDISH CRÊPES ❖

This special recipe is a family favorite for weekend and vacation breakfasts!

3	eggs	3
3 cups	skim milk	750 mL
2 cups	all-purpose flour	500 mL
1/4 cup	diet margarine, melted	60 mL
1 tsp.	vegetable oil	5 mL
3/4 tsp.	salt	3 mL
1/4 cup	SPLENDA® Granular	60 mL
	vegetable oil	

Yogurt Cheese:

2 cups	skim milk yogurt	500 mL

Beat the eggs well. Add the remaining ingredients and beat until smooth. Bake on a hot, nonstick frying pan. A wok or a crêpe pan will produce very symmetrical crêpes. Brush the pan with a little vegetable oil. Pour by the 1/4 cupfuls (60 mL). Turn when bubbles form and cook until lightly golden. **Yield: approximately 20 crêpes.**

Yogurt Cheese: Line a colander with coffee filter paper. Place the colander over a bowl. Pour skim milk yogurt into the colander and cover. Refrigerate for 6 hours or overnight. Discard the liquid in the bowl and put the yogurt cheese in a closed container. Refrigerate up to 1 week.

❖ Try serving these crêpes by spreading lightly with yogurt cheese or chilled custard sauce, page 81, roll up and pour 1 of the fruit sauces of your choice, pages 82 and 83, over each crêpe. Garnish with a dollop of Sugarless Whipped Topping, page 11. If preferred, top the crêpes with fresh fruit, such as strawberries, blueberries, sliced peaches, etc., and Sugarless Whipped Topping.

❖ If saving time is important, commercial low-calorie whipped topping is available and may be substituted for Sugarless Whipped Topping in any of these recipes.

❖ SWEDISH WAFFLES OR PANCAKES ❖

Great for dessert and for breakfast too.

2	eggs, beaten	2
2 cups	all-purpose flour	500 mL
1 tbsp.	baking powder	15 mL
1/3 cup	SPLENDA® Granular	75 mL
1/2 tsp.	salt	2 mL
1/4 cup	diet margarine, softened	60 mL
1 3/4 cups	skim milk	425 mL

Beat the eggs. Add the remaining ingredients and beat until smooth.

Waffles: Use a waffle iron. Serve with a fruit sauce of your choice, pages 82 and 83 and a dollop of Sugarless Whipped Topping below, if desired. **Yield: 16 waffles.**

Pancakes: Use a greased, hot, nonstick frying pan and drop batter by 1/4 cupfuls (60 mL). Cook until golden on both sides. Serve with diet margarine and low-calorie jam or as above. **Yield: 15 pancakes.**

VARIATION: Blueberry Pancakes — Fold 2 cups (500 mL) fresh blueberries into the batter.

❖ SUGARLESS WHIPPED TOPPING ❖

A lovely alternative to commercial whipped toppings and a low-fat, low-cholesterol substitute for whipped cream, it has excellent holding power. Keep the garnished dessert refrigerated.

1 1/2 tsp.	unflavored gelatin	7 mL
1/4 cup	cold water	60 mL
3/4 cup	ice cold water	175 mL
3/4 cup	skim milk powder	175 mL
2 tbsp.	vegetable oil	30 mL
1 tsp.	lemon juice	5 mL
1/4 cup	SPLENDA® Granular	60 mL

In a small saucepan, soak the gelatin in the 1/4 cup (60 mL) cold water for 1 minute. Heat to dissolve. Set aside to cool to room temperature. In a chilled bowl, with chilled beaters, beat together ice cold water and milk powder until thickened. With the machine running, add remaining ingredients. Beat another 3 minutes. Cover and freeze for 15 minutes; stir then refrigerate. **Yield: 3 cups (750 mL).**

❖ SCONES ❖

Light and flaky scones with jam are perfect for tea.

2 cups	all-purpose flour	500 mL
1/2 cup	SPLENDA® Granular	125 mL
1 tbsp.	baking powder	15 mL
3/4 tsp.	salt	3 mL
1/3 cup	cold butter OR margarine	75 mL
1	egg	1
2/3 cup	skim milk	150 mL
	skim milk for brushing tops	
1 tbsp.	SPLENDA® Granular	15 mL

Sift the dry ingredients into a medium-sized bowl. Cut in the butter until the mixture resembles breadcrumbs.

Beat the egg slightly and add the skim milk. Stir into the dry ingredients until just mixed.

Pat or roll dough into 2, 6" (15 cm) circles. Score the tops of circles into 6 wedges and brush with milk. Sprinkle with SPLENDA® Granular.

Bake on a greased baking sheet in a 425°F (220°C) oven for 15 minutes. Cut into wedges, split and spread with diet margarine and your favorite low-calorie jam. **Yield: 12 scones.**

❖ PINEAPPLE RASPBERRY MUFFINS ❖

A wonderful blend of fruit flavors.

2 cups	all-purpose flour	500 mL
3/4 cup	SPLENDA® Granular	175 mL
1 tbsp.	baking powder	15 mL
1/2 tsp.	salt	2 mL
2	eggs	2
1 cup	nondairy 1% soy beverage OR skim milk	250 mL
1/4 cup	vegetable oil	60 mL
1 tsp.	lemon juice	5 mL
1/4 cup	drained, unsweetened, crushed pineapple	60 mL
1 cup	frozen, unsweetened raspberries	250 mL

❖ PINEAPPLE RASPBERRY MUFFINS ❖

Continued

Sift the dry ingredients together.

Beat the eggs, soy beverage (or skim milk), vegetable oil and lemon juice together. Stir in the crushed pineapple.

Add the semiliquid ingredients to the dry ingredients and stir just until moistened. Carefully fold in the frozen raspberries.

Fill 12 greased muffin cups ³/₄ full. Bake at 400°F (200°C) for approximately 15 minutes, or until a knife inserted in the center of the muffins comes out clean. **Yield: 12 muffins**.

See photograph on page 17.

❖ LARGE BLUEBERRY MUFFINS ❖

Gorgeous, showy muffins.

3 cups	all-purpose flour	750 mL
2 tbsp.	baking powder	30 mL
1 tsp.	salt	5 mL
1 cup	SPLENDA® Granular	250 mL
2 cups	frozen, unsweetened blueberries	500 mL
¹/₃ cup	margarine, softened	75 mL
2	eggs	2
2 cups	skim milk	500 mL
2 tsp.	vanilla	10 mL

Sift the dry ingredients together. Stir in the frozen blueberries.

Cream the margarine and add the eggs, milk and vanilla, beating well. Stir into the flour mixture, just until moist.

Fill 12 greased muffin cups to the top and bake in a 375°F (190°C) oven for 20 minutes. If smaller muffins are desired, fill 18 greased muffin cups ³/₄ full and bake for 15 minutes. Refrigerate or freeze muffins. Warm in the microwave oven before serving. **Yield: 12-18 muffins.**

See photograph on page 17.

❖ APPLE CINNAMON ❖ STREUSEL MUFFINS

Looks and tastes wonderful, with pieces of apple throughout.

2	eggs	2
1/4 cup	vegetable oil	60 mL
1 1/4 cups	sour skim milk (include 1 tbsp. [15 mL] vinegar to sour the milk)	300 mL
1 1/2 cups	finely diced apples	375 mL
1 3/4 cups	all-purpose flour	425 mL
1 tsp.	baking soda	5 mL
2 tsp.	baking powder	10 mL
1 tsp.	cinnamon	5 mL
1/2 tsp.	salt	2 mL
3/4 cup	SPLENDA® Granular	175 mL

Streusel Topping:

1/4 cup	all-purpose flour	60 mL
1/2 cup	SPLENDA® Granular	125 mL
1/4 cup	margarine	60 mL

Beat the eggs well. Stir in the vegetable oil, the sour milk and the diced apples.

Sift the dry ingredients together. Set aside.

Streusel Topping: Combine the all-purpose flour and SPLENDA® Granular. Rub in the margarine.

Pour the semiliquid ingredients into a well made in the center of the dry ingredients. Stir quickly just until moistened. Spoon the muffin mixture into 18 greased muffin cups, 3/4 full and sprinkle with the streusel topping. Bake at 350°F (180°C) for approximately 15 minutes, or until a knife inserted in the muffins comes out clean. **Yield: 18 muffins.**

❖ BANANA OATMEAL MUFFINS ❖

A healthy muffin for everyday.

1 cup	skim milk	250 mL
1 cup	rolled oats	250 mL
2 cups	blended bread flour	500 mL
5 tsp.	baking powder	25 mL
1 tsp.	baking soda	5 mL
1 tsp.	salt	5 mL
1/2 tsp.	cinnamon	2 mL
3/4 cup	SPLENDA® Granular	175 mL
5	medium bananas	5
2	eggs	2
1/3 cup	diet margarine	75 mL
2 tsp.	vanilla	10 mL

Pour the milk over the oats and set aside.

Sift the flour and remaining dry ingredients together in a large bowl.

Mash the bananas and set aside.

Beat the eggs, margarine and vanilla. Stir into the oats and milk mixture.

Add this semiliquid mixture to a well in the center of the dry ingredients. Scoop the bananas into the well too. Stir only until the flour is moistened. Fill 18 greased muffin cups ¾ full. Bake at 375°F (190°C) for approximately 20 minutes. **Yield: 18 muffins.**

❖ Blended bread flour is a commercially available blend of whole-wheat and white flours. It is used as a healthy alternative to white flour.

❖ CHOCOLATE CHEESECAKE ❖ MUFFINS

A muffin for chocolate lovers.

Cream Cheese Mixture:

3 oz.	light cream cheese, softened	85 g
2 tbsp.	SPLENDA® Granular	30 mL

Chocolate Batter:

1¹/₂ cups	all-purpose flour	375 mL
³/₄ cup	SPLENDA® Granular	175 mL
3 tbsp.	cocoa	45 mL
1 tbsp.	baking powder	15 mL
¹/₂ tsp.	salt	2 mL
1	egg	1
1 cup	skim milk	250 mL
¹/₃ cup	vegetable oil	75 mL
	icing (confectioner's) sugar (optional)	

Cream Cheese Mixture: Beat the cream cheese and 2 tbsp. (30 mL) SPLENDA® Granular until smooth and light. Set aside.

Chocolate Batter: Sift the dry ingredients together in a large bowl. Make a well in the center.

Beat the egg very well. Stir in the skim milk and vegetable oil.

Add the liquid ingredients to the well in the center of the dry ingredients. Stir just until moistened.

Spoon a little chocolate batter into the bottom of 8 greased muffin cups. Place a generous teaspoon (5 mL) of the cream cheese mixture on top of the batter in each muffin cup and top with more chocolate batter, to ³/₄ full.

Bake in a 375°F (190°C) oven for 20 minutes. Dust with icing sugar, if desired. **Yield: 8 muffins.**

Large Blueberry Muffins, page 13
Pineapple Raspberry Muffins, page 12
Apple Cinnamon Coffeecake, page 26
Cranberry Orange Loaf, page 21
Peach Yogurt Shake, page 9
Strawberry Yogurt Shake, page 9

❖ APPLE CINNAMON SWIRL LOAF ❖

A large, moist loaf with a marbled cinnamon swirl.

1 cup	skim milk	250 mL
1 tbsp.	white vinegar OR lemon juice	15 mL
2 cups	all-purpose flour	500 mL
1 cup	SPLENDA® Granular	250 mL
1 tsp.	salt	5 mL
1¹/₂ tsp.	cinnamon	7 mL
2 tsp.	baking powder	10 mL
¹/₂ tsp.	baking soda	2 mL
¹/₄ cup	vegetable oil	60 mL
2	eggs	2
1 tsp.	vanilla	5 mL
¹/₂ cup	unsweetened apple juice	125 mL
Topping:		
2 tbsp.	SPLENDA® Granular	30 mL
1 tsp.	cinnamon	5 mL
1 tbsp.	all-purpose flour	15 mL
2 tsp.	margarine	10 mL

To make sour skim milk, add white vinegar or lemon juice to the milk to measure 1 cup (250 mL). Set aside.

Sift the dry ingredients into a mixing bowl. Add the remaining ingredients, including the sour milk, and beat until smooth. Pour into a greased 3 x 5 x 9" (7 x 13 x 23 cm) loaf pan

Topping: Mix SPLENDA® Granular, cinnamon and flour together and rub in the margarine. Sprinkle over the loaf and swirl in with a knife.

Bake at 350°F (180°C) for 30-45 minutes. Allow the loaf to cool for 10 minutes. Loosen the edges with a knife and invert, shaking lightly. Allow to cool on a cake rack. **Yield: 1 loaf.**

❖ APPLESAUCE NUT BREAD ❖

Use the sugarless applesauce recipe on page 83.

2	eggs	2
1/4 cup	vegetable oil	60 mL
2/3 cup	skim milk	150 mL
1 cup	SPLENDA® Granular	250 mL
1 cup	applesauce, page 83	250 mL
2 cups	all-purpose flour	500 mL
1/2 tsp.	baking powder	2 mL
1 tsp.	baking soda	5 mL
1/2 tsp.	cinnamon	2 mL
1/4 tsp.	salt	1 mL
1/8 tsp.	nutmeg	0.5 mL
1/2 cup	chopped pecans	125 mL

In a mixing bowl, beat together the eggs, oil, milk and SPLENDA® Granular. Add the applesauce and beat 30 seconds.

Sift the dry ingredients together in another bowl. Stir in the chopped pecans. Add the liquid ingredients and stir just until moistened.

Spoon into a greased 3 x 5 x 9" (7 x 13 x 23 cm) loaf pan and bake at 350°F (180°C) for approximately 40 minutes, or until a knife inserted in the middle of the loaf comes out clean. **Yield: 1 loaf.**

❖ If the applesauce is chunky, bits of apple will be visible in the loaf.

❖ BANANA LOAF ❖

A good old standby — kids love banana loaf.

2/3 cup	margarine	150 mL
4	eggs	4
2 tsp.	vanilla	10 mL
1/2 cup	skim milk	125 mL
4 cups	all-purpose flour OR blended flour	1 L
2 tbsp.	baking powder	30 mL
1 tsp.	salt	5 mL
1 1/2 cups	SPLENDA® Granular	375 mL
6	medium bananas, mashed	6

❖ BANANA LOAF ❖

Continued

Combine and beat the margarine, eggs and vanilla well. Stir in the milk.

Sift all the dry ingredients into a large bowl. Add the liquid ingredients as well as the mashed bananas. Stir quickly, just until moistened. Scoop into 2 greased 3 x 5 x 9" (7 x 13 x 23 cm) loaf pans.

Bake in a 350°F (180°C) oven for approximately 40 minutes, or until a knife inserted in the center comes out clean. **Yield: 2 large loaves.**

❖ CRANBERRY ORANGE LOAF ❖

This moist colorful loaf has a fabulous flavor.

1/4 cup	margarine OR butter	60 mL
1	egg	1
1 1/4 cups	SPLENDA® Granular	300 mL
1 1/2 cups	juice of 1 orange and water to equal	375 mL
2 cups	all-purpose flour	500 mL
2 tsp.	baking powder	10 mL
1/2 tsp.	baking soda	2 mL
1/4 tsp.	salt	1 mL
3 tbsp.	grated orange rind	45 mL
1 2/3 cups	frozen, unsweetened cranberries	400 mL

Cream the margarine; add the egg and SPLENDA® Granular. Beat well. Stir in the orange juice/water mixture.

Sift the flour, baking powder, baking soda and salt together. Stir in the orange rind and cranberries. Combine the liquid and dry ingredients, stirring just until moistened. Pour into greased 3 x 5 x 9" (7 x 13 x 23 cm) loaf pan.

Bake at 350°F (180°C) for approximately 50 minutes, or until lightly browned and a knife inserted in the center comes out clean. Allow to cool 10 minutes, loosen the edges and remove loaf from pan. Refrigerate to prolong the freshness. **Yield: 1 loaf.**

See photograph on page 17.

❖ EASY CINNAMON-SWIRL ❖
YEAST LOAF

The taste of cinnamon buns without the high calories.

1/2 cup	skim milk	125 mL
1/4 cup	butter OR margarine	60 mL
1/4 cup	unsweetened applesauce	60 mL
3 1/4 cups	all-purpose flour	810 mL
1/4 cup	SPLENDA® Granular	60 mL
1 tsp.	salt	5 mL
1 tbsp.	instant yeast	15 mL
2	eggs, lightly beaten	2

Filling:

1 cup	SPLENDA® Granular	250 mL
1/4 cup	all-purpose flour	60 mL
2 tsp.	cinnamon	10 mL
1/4 cup	butter OR margarine	60 mL
1/4 cup	chopped pecans (optional)	60 mL
1/4 cup	raisins (optional)	60 mL
2 tbsp.	diet margarine, softened	30 mL

Glaze:

1	egg yolk	1
1 tbsp.	skim milk	15 mL

Heat the milk to 125-130°F (50-55°C). With a food processor on low speed, beat the margarine, applesauce, flour, SPLENDA® Granular, salt and yeast. Add the eggs and milk alternately through the feed tube until a dough ball forms. On a floured surface, knead dough a few minutes. Place in a greased bowl, cover with a damp towel, and allow to rest for 10 minutes. Preheat oven to 200°F (100°C) and switch off.

Filling: Meanwhile, combine the first 3 filling ingredients and rub in the butter. Stir in the pecans and raisins. Roll the dough to a 9 x 12" (23 x 30 cm) rectangle. Spread with margarine and sprinkle with filling, leaving a 1/2" (1.3 cm) border. Roll up jelly-roll style from the long end. Place loaf on a greased baking sheet. Cover with a damp towel, place in the oven and allow to double in size, about 1 hour.

Glaze: Brush the loaf with the lightly beaten egg and milk.

Bake at 375°F (190°C) for 20 minutes. **Yield: 1 loaf, 16 servings**

❖ ZUCCHINI ALMOND COFFEECAKE ❖

A healthy, moist cake with great flavor.

2¹/₂ cups	all-purpose flour	625 mL
2 tsp.	baking powder	10 mL
1 tsp.	baking soda	5 mL
3/4 tsp.	salt	3 mL
1 tsp.	cinnamon	5 mL
2	eggs	2
¹/₃ cup	vegetable oil	75 mL
1¹/₃ cups	SPLENDA® Granular	325 mL
1¹/₂ cups	grated, unpeeled zucchini, lightly drained	375 mL
¹/₂ cup	unsweetened apple juice	125 mL
1 tsp.	almond flavoring	5 mL

Almond Cream Cheese Icing:

³/₄ cup	low-fat cottage cheese	175 mL
2 oz.	light cream cheese, softened	60 g
2 tbsp.	diet margarine	30 mL
¹/₃ cup	SPLENDA® Granular	75 mL
¹/₈ tsp.	almond flavoring	0.5 mL
	slivered, blanched almonds for garnish	

Sift the first 5 dry ingredients together in a large bowl.

Beat the eggs well. Add the vegetable oil and SPLENDA® Granular. Beat again. Stir in the grated zucchini, apple juice and almond flavoring.

Add the semiliquid ingredients to the dry ingredients and stir just until moistened. Scoop into a greased 9 x 13" (23 x 33 cm) pan. Bake at 350°F (180°C) for approximately 35 minutes. Cool.

Almond Cream Cheese Icing: Use a blender or a food processor with a sharp blade to process the cottage cheese until very smooth. Add the cream cheese, margarine, SPLENDA® Granular and almond flavoring, beating again. Spread the icing on the cooled zucchini cake and cut into 24 squares. Garnish each square with slivered almonds.
Yield: 24 squares.

❖ STRAWBERRY STREUSEL ❖
COFFEECAKE

This special coffeecake is similar to some European cakes.

Filling:

1/2 cup	reserved strawberry juice OR water	125 mL
2 1/2 tbsp.	cornstarch	40 mL
3 cups	fresh OR frozen, unsweetened, sliced, thawed, drained strawberries	750 mL
1/2 cup	SPLENDA® Granular	125 mL
2 drops	red food coloring (optional)	2 drops

Cake Batter:

2 3/4 cups	cake and pastry flour	675 mL
3/4 cup	SPLENDA® Granular	175 mL
2/3 cup	butter OR margarine	150 mL
1/3 cup	sliced, blanched almonds	75 mL
1 tsp.	baking powder	5 mL
1/2 tsp.	baking soda	2 mL
2	eggs	2
1 tsp.	vanilla	5 mL
1 cup	skim milk	250 mL

Filling: In a saucepan, gradually stir the juice or water into the cornstarch until smooth. Add sliced strawberries and SPLENDA® Granular. Over medium heat, cook and stir until the sauce thickens. Add a couple of drops of red food coloring.

Cake Batter: Combine the cake and pastry flour with SPLENDA® Granular and rub in the butter or margarine until crumbly. Combine 1/2 cup (125 mL) of the flour mixture with the almonds and set aside. Add the baking powder and baking soda to the remaining flour mixture.

Beat the eggs, vanilla and skim milk together. Pour into a well in the center of the dry ingredients and stir just until moistened. Using 2/3 of the batter, spread over a greased 8 or 9" (20 or 23 cm) springform pan to form a crust. The center should be lower than the sides. Sides should reach up 3/4" (2 cm) all around. Pour the strawberry filling in the center. Using the remaining 1/3 of the batter, drop spoonfuls over the filling. Sprinkle the reserved almond mixture overall. Bake in a 350°F (180°C) oven for approximately 25 minutes, or until a knife inserted in the cake portion comes out clean. **Serves 8.**

BLUEBERRY STREUSEL ❖ COFFEECAKE

A super coffeecake — packed with blueberries.

2¹/4 cups	cake and pastry flour	550 mL
2 tsp.	baking powder	10 mL
1 tsp.	baking soda	5 mL
1/2 tsp.	salt	2 mL
1 cup	SPLENDA® Granular	250 mL
2 cups	fresh OR frozen, unsweetened blueberries	500 mL
2	eggs	2
¹/4 cup	vegetable oil	60 mL
1¹/3 cups	skim milk	325 mL
1 tsp.	vanilla	5 mL

Streusel Topping:

¹/4 cup	all-purpose flour	60 mL
¹/3 cup	SPLENDA® Granular	75 mL
¹/2 tsp.	cinnamon	2 mL
¹/4 cup	margarine	60 mL

Sift the flour, baking powder, baking soda and salt together in a large bowl. Stir in the SPLENDA® Granular. Fold in the blueberries. Beat the eggs well, stirring in the vegetable oil, skim milk and vanilla.

Streusel Topping: Combine the first 3 ingredients and mix well. Rub in the margarine. Set aside.

Add the liquid ingredients to the dry ingredients, stirring just until moistened. Pour into a 9 x 13" (23 x 33 cm) greased baking pan. Sprinkle the streusel topping over the cake batter. Bake at 350°F (180°C) for 20 minutes, or until a knife inserted in the coffeecake comes out clean. **Cut into 24 squares.**

❖ To preserve freshness, refrigerate the coffeecake. Warm in the microwave oven before serving.

❖ APPLE CINNAMON COFFEECAKE ❖

A special version of a favorite flavor combination.
My sons love this.

2²/₃ cups	all-purpose flour	650 mL
1¹/₂ cups	SPLENDA® Granular	375 mL
2 tbsp.	baking powder	30 mL
³/₄ tsp.	salt	3 mL
¹/₂ cup	butter OR margarine	125 mL
2	eggs	2
1¹/₂ cups	skim milk	375 mL
2 tsp.	vanilla	10 mL
4	cooking apples, peeled and sliced	4

Topping:

¹/₃ cup	SPLENDA® Granular	75 mL
¹/₂ tsp.	cinnamon	2 mL

Sift the dry ingredients together. Rub in the butter until the mixture resembles fine breadcrumbs.

Beat the eggs well. Stir in the milk and vanilla. Add the liquid ingredients to the dry ingredients and stir just until moistened.

Turn out into a greased 9 x 13" (23 x 33 cm) baking pan. Push the apples well into the batter.

Topping: Stir the topping ingredients together well. Sprinkle the cake batter with the topping and bake at 350°F (180°C) for approximately 25 minutes, or until a knife inserted in the middle comes out clean. **Cut into 24 squares.**

See photograph on page 17.

❖ WHITE CAKE ❖

This lovely, light-textured cake rises very high.

1³/₄ cups	skim milk	425mL
1 tbsp.	vinegar	15 mL
2¹/₂ cups	self-raising cake flour	625 mL
2 tsp.	baking powder	10 mL
¹/₂ tsp.	baking soda	2 mL
1³/₄ cups	SPLENDA® Granular	425 mL
¹/₂ cup	shortening, butter OR margarine	125 mL
3	eggs	3
1 tsp.	vanilla	5 mL
1-2 tbsp.	sweetened condensed milk (may be omitted, but the cake will not rise as high)	15-30 mL

Preheat the oven to 350°F (180°C). To make sour milk, add 1 tbsp. (15 mL) white vinegar to the skim milk to measure 1³/₄ cups (425 mL). Set aside. Sift the dry ingredients together.

Cream the shortening, adding the eggs and vanilla. Beat well. Stir in the sweetened condensed milk.

To the egg mixture, add the dry ingredients and sour skim milk simultaneously in 3 additions, beating 30 seconds to 1 minute after each addition, until smooth.

Pour equally into 2 greased 8" (20 cm) round cake pans and smooth lightly with the back of a spoon for even distribution. Bake 20 minutes, or until a knife inserted in the cake comes out clean. Do not open the oven until at least 10 minutes of baking time has passed.

Cool on a cake rack. Ice with a frosting of your choice. If you wish, garnish with strawberry or other fresh fruit slices. **Serves 12.**

See photograph on the back cover.

VARIATION: Marble Cake — Set aside ³/₄ cup (175 mL) of the cake batter and stir in 4 tsp. (20 mL) cocoa powder, 2 tbsp. (30 mL) SPLENDA® Granular and 2 tbsp. (30 mL) skim milk. Drop blobs of chocolate batter over the plain batter in each of the cake pans and use a knife to create a swirl effect. Bake and frost as above.

❖ ORANGE MANDARIN CAKE ❖

Wonderful flavor of southern sunshine.

1/2 cup	shortening, softened	125 mL
3	eggs	3
1 tbsp.	finely grated orange rind (optional)	15 mL
2 1/2 cups	self-raising cake flour	625 mL
2 tsp.	baking powder	10 mL
1/2 tsp.	baking soda	2 mL
1 3/4 cups	SPLENDA® Granular	425 mL
1/2 cup	water	125 mL
1 1/4 cups	fresh orange juice OR juice from concentrate	300 mL

Filling and Topping:

Orange Frosting, page 80
fresh orange slices OR canned mandarin
orange segments

Preheat the oven to 350°F (180°C). Cream the shortening, then add the eggs, beating well. Stir in the orange rind.

Sift the dry ingredients together.

Stir the water into the orange juice. To the egg mixture, add the dry ingredients and the orange juice simultaneously in 3 additions, beating 30 seconds to 1 minute after each addition, until smooth.

Pour into 2 greased 8" (20 cm) round cake pans and smooth lightly with the back of a spoon for even distribution. Bake 15-20 minutes.

Invert gently onto wire racks and cool thoroughly before frosting the cake.

Filling and Topping: Fill and ice the whole cake with Orange Frosting, page 80. Garnish with fresh orange slices or mandarin orange segments, if desired. **Serves 12.**

❖ BLACK FOREST CAKE ❖

A special occasion dessert. My mother cannot resist this cake.

5 tbsp.	shortening, softened	75 mL
4	eggs yolks	4
1¹/₄ cups	cake flour	300 mL
¹/₃ cup	cocoa	75 mL
³/₄ cup	SPLENDA® Granular	175 mL
2 tsp.	baking powder	10 mL
4	egg whites	4
¹/₂ tsp.	cream of tartar	2 mL
1 cup	unsweetened apple juice	250 mL

Filling and Topping:

3 tbsp.	kirsch liqueur OR see variations below	45 mL
2 cups	whipping cream	500 mL
2 tsp.	cornstarch	10 mL
1 tsp.	vanilla	5 mL
¹/₄ cup	cocoa (optional)	60 mL
¹/₄ cup	SPLENDA® Granular	60 mL
1¹/₄ cups	pitted fresh OR canned cherries	300 mL
¹/₂ oz.	semisweet baking chocolate (optional)	15 g
	fresh OR bottled cherries with stems	

Preheat the oven to 350°F (180°C). Cream shortening; add egg yolks. Beat well. Sift dry ingredients together. Beat the egg whites until stiff, adding cream of tartar. Set aside. To egg yolk mixture, add the dry ingredients and apple juice simultaneously in 3 additions, beating 1 minute after each addition, until smooth. Fold the egg whites into the cake batter and spoon equal amounts into 3 greased 8" (20 cm) round cake pans. Bake approximately 15-20 minutes. Allow to cool on cake racks.

Filling and Topping: Sprinkle cake layers with kirsch. Whip cream with cornstarch until thick. Beat in vanilla, cocoa and SPLENDA® Granular. Spread ¹/₃ of the cream on the first cake layer and place pitted cherries around perimeter and in the center. Repeat with next 2 layers. Garnish top of cake with chocolate shavings and stemmed cherries. Refrigerate cake if not serving immediately. **Serves 12.**

VARIATIONS: Substitute for the kirsch, 2 tbsp. (30 mL) unsweetened pineapple juice, 1 tbsp. (15 mL) SPLENDA® Granular and ¹/₂ tsp. (2 mL) brandy extract or use artificial kirsch flavoring.

See photograph on page 71.

❖ CHOCOLATE CAKE ❖

Moist and airy.

¹/₂ cup	shortening, softened	125 mL
3	eggs	3
2¹/₄ cups	self-raising cake flour	550 mL
1³/₄ cups	SPLENDA® Granular	425 mL
¹/₄ cup	cocoa powder	60 mL
2 tsp.	baking powder	10 mL
¹/₂ tsp.	baking soda	2 mL
¹/₂ cup	water	125 mL
1¹/₄ cups	unsweetened apple juice	300 mL

Filling and Topping

Chocolate Cream Frosting, page 79, OR
Chocolate Pudding Icing, page 79
halved strawberries OR red candied
 cherries for garnish, if desired
chocolate shavings (optional)

Preheat the oven to 350°F (180°C). Cream the shortening. Add the eggs and beat well.

Sift the dry ingredients together.

Combine the water and apple juice. To the egg mixture, add the dry ingredients and the apple juice mixture simultaneously in three additions, beating 30 seconds to 1 minute after each addition until smooth.

Pour equal amounts into 2 greased 8" (20 cm) round cake pans and smooth lightly with the back of a spoon for even distribution. Bake for 15-20 minutes. Invert gently onto wire racks and allow to cool thoroughly before attempting to frost the cake.

Filling and Topping: Fill and ice the whole cake with a frosting of your choice. Garnish with halved strawberries or cherries and/or chocolate shavings, if desired. **Serves 12.**

❖ CARROT CAKE ❖

A wonderfully moist high cake.

2 cups	all-purpose flour	500 mL
1 tbsp.	baking powder	15 mL
1/2 tsp.	salt	2 mL
1 1/2 cups	SPLENDA® Granular	375 mL
1/4 cup	chopped walnuts (optional)	60 mL
2	eggs	2
1/4 cup	vegetable oil	60 mL
1 1/2 cups	finely grated carrots	375 mL
1/2 cup	drained, unsweetened, crushed pineapple	125 mL
1/2 cup	unsweetened pineapple juice	125 mL
1/2 cup	water	125 mL

Cream Cheese Icing:

1/2 cup	low-fat cottage cheese	125 mL
1/2 cup	light cream cheese, softened (3 oz. [85 g])	125 mL
2 tbsp.	diet margarine	30 mL
1/4 cup	SPLENDA® Granular	60 mL

Preheat the oven to 350°F (180°C). Sift all the dry ingredients together. Stir in the walnuts.

Beat the eggs well and stir in the vegetable oil. Add the carrots, crushed pineapple, pineapple juice and water.

Add the semiliquid ingredients to a well in the center of the dry ingredients. Stir only until moistened. Spoon into a greased 8" (20 cm) or 9" (23 cm) square baking pan and bake approximately 25 minutes, or until a knife inserted in the cake comes out clean. If a brownie-style carrot cake is preferred, spoon the cake batter into 2 greased 8" (20 cm) square baking pans. Test for doneness after 20 minutes.

Cream Cheese Icing: In a food processor or blender with a sharp blade, process the cottage cheese until smooth. Add the cream cheese, diet margarine and SPLENDA® Granular. Beat until smooth. Cut the carrot cake into squares and frost with the cream cheese icing. Place a walnut on each square. Otherwise, instead of the Cream Cheese Icing, dust with icing sugar for a decorative touch. **Serves 9.**

❖ This recipe doubles easily and freezes well.

❖ BANANA CHIFFON CAKE ❖

A light tube cake smothered in gooey chocolate nut sauce.

2 cups	self-raising cake and pastry flour	500 mL
1 cup	SPLENDA® Granular	250 mL
1 tsp.	baking powder	5 mL
1 tsp.	baking soda	5 mL
2	egg whites	2
1/4 tsp.	cream of tartar	1 mL
1/3 cup	SPLENDA® Granular	75 mL
1/3 cup	vegetable oil	75 mL
1 cup	mashed, ripe bananas	250 mL
2/3 cup	skim milk (including 2 tsp. [10 mL] lemon juice)	150 mL
1 1/2 tsp.	vanilla	7 mL
2	egg yolks	2

Chocolate Nut Sauce:

3 tbsp.	all-purpose flour	45 mL
1 tbsp.	cocoa	15 mL
1 cup	SPLENDA® Granular	250 mL
2 tbsp.	diet margarine, melted	30 mL
1 cup	skim milk	250 mL
1 tsp.	vanilla	5 mL
1/2 cup	chopped nuts	125 mL

Cake Batter: Preheat the oven to 350°F (180°C). Sift together the flour, SPLENDA® Granular, baking powder and baking soda. Beat egg whites for 30 seconds; add cream of tartar; beat another 2 minutes, adding SPLENDA® Granular towards the end. Set aside. Combine oil, bananas, half of the soured milk and vanilla. Add to the flour mixture and beat 1 minute. Add remaining sour milk and egg yolks. Beat another minute. Fold in beaten egg whites. Pour into an ungreased 9" (23 cm) tube springform or a greased regular tube pan.

Bake 30 minutes, until a knife inserted in the cake comes out clean. If cake browns too quickly, reduce heat to 300°F (150°C) during the last 5 minutes. Cool by inverting over a funnel for 1 hour. Remove cake and frost with cooled Chocolate Nut Sauce.

Chocolate Nut Sauce: Combine dry ingredients and margarine in a saucepan. Gradually stir in milk. Cook over medium heat until thickened. Stir in vanilla and nuts; keep a few nuts for garnish. **Serves 10-12.**

❖ LEMON ALMOND CHEESECAKE ❖

Delicious combination of citrus and nuts.

Almond Crumb Crust:

1 cup	graham cracker crumbs	250 mL
1/2 cup	almonds, finely ground	125 mL
1/4 cup	SPLENDA® Granular	60 mL
1/3 cup+1 tbsp.	diet margarine, melted	90 mL

Filling:

2 cups	low-fat ricotta cheese	500 mL
3	eggs	3
8 oz.	light cream cheese, softened	250 g
1 cup	skim milk yogurt	250 mL
1 1/4 cups	SPLENDA® Granular	300 mL
2 tbsp.	all-purpose flour (optional)*	30 mL
1 tsp.	vanilla	5 mL
1/2 tsp.	salt	2 mL
1/3 cup	lemon juice	75 mL
1 tbsp.	finely-grated lemon rind (optional)	15 mL
2 drops	yellow food coloring (optional)	2 drops

Topping:

sliced, blanched almonds

Crust: Combine the crust ingredients. Press over the bottom of a deep 9" (23 cm) glass pie dish and about 1 1/4" (3 cm) up the sides. Set aside.

Filling: In a blender or food processor with a sharp blade, process the ricotta cheese until smooth. Add the eggs and cream cheese. Beat until smooth. Add the yogurt, SPLENDA® Granular, all-purpose flour, vanilla, salt, lemon juice, grated lemon peel and yellow food color. Beat until well blended.

Pour the cream cheese mixture over the graham cracker crust. Bake in a 350°F (180°C) oven for 35-45 minutes, or until the center is set.

Topping: Garnish with sliced, blanched almonds. If desired, use a commercial low-calorie dessert topping or the Sugarless Whipped Topping, page 11, before sprinkling with the almonds. Refrigerate until well-chilled. **Serves 10-12.**

* Adding the flour produces a thicker, more dense consistency, whereas omitting it produces a smooth, creamy texture.

❖ ORANGE MANDARIN CHEESECAKE ❖

A simply delicious variation of the Lemon Almond Cheesecake.

Crust:

	Crumb Crust, page 37, OR Sugarless Sweet Dough Crust, page 45	

Filling:

	ingredients for Lemon Almond Cheesecake, page 33, except for the last 3 filling ingredients, substitute	
¹/₃ cup	orange juice	75 mL
1 tbsp.	grated orange rind (optional)	15 mL
2 drops	orange food coloring (optional)	2 drops

Topping:

2 cups	commercial low-calorie dessert topping OR Sugarless Whipped Topping, page 11	500 mL
	fresh orange slices or canned mandarin orange segments, drained, for garnish	

Follow the ingredients and method for Lemon Almond Cheesecake, page 33, except use the above filling ingredients to replace the last 3 filling ingredients. Prepare topping. Spread on the cheesecake and garnish. Serves 10-12.

❖ LIME CHEESECAKE ❖

A fresh lime variation of the Orange Mandarin Cheesecake above.

Crust:

	Crumb Crust, page 37, OR Sugarless Sweet Dough Crust, page 45	

Filling:

¹/₃ cup	lime juice	75 mL
1 tbsp.	grated lime rind (optional)	15 mL
2 drops	green food coloring (optional)	2 drops

Follow the ingredients and method for the Lemon Almond Cheesecake, page 33, except use the above ingredients to replace the last 3 filling ingredients. Garnish as above, using lime slices if desired. **Serves 10-12.** See photograph opposite.

34

❖ RASPBERRY LEMON CHEESECAKE ❖

A thick rich-tasting cheesecake with a flavorful topping

Low-Fat Crumb Crust: (Grape-Nuts have no added sugar)

2/3 cup	Grape-Nuts cereal OR graham crumbs	150 mL
2/3 cup	graham cracker crumbs	150 mL
1/3 cup	SPLENDA® Granular	75 mL
1 tbsp.	butter OR margarine, melted	15 mL
1	egg white, beaten until frothy	1
1 tbsp.	unsweetened apple juice OR water	15 mL

Filling:

2 cups	low-fat ricotta cheese	500 mL
8 oz.	light cream cheese, softened	250 g
3	eggs	3
1 cup	skim milk yogurt	250 mL
1/2 cup	light sour cream	125 mL
1/3 cup	all-purpose flour	75 mL
1/4 cup	lemon juice	60 mL
1 tbsp.	grated lemon rind (optional)	15 mL
1 1/4 cups	SPLENDA® Granular	300 mL
1/4 tsp.	salt	1 mL

Raspberry Topping:

1/2 cup	reserved raspberry juice	125 mL
3 tbsp.	cornstarch	45 mL
2/3 cup	SPLENDA® Granular	150 mL
2 x 10 oz.	pkg. frozen, unsweetened raspberries, thawed and drained	2 x 285 g

Crust: In a blender, process Grape Nuts into crumbs. Combine all ingredients. Press into a 9" (23 cm) springform pan. Bake at 350°F (180°C) for 10 minutes. Cool. **OR,** use Sugarless Sweet Dough Crust, page 45.

Filling: In a food processor or blender with a sharp blade, process ricotta cheese until smooth. Add cream cheese and eggs. Beat. Add the remaining ingredients. Beat until smooth. Pour over the graham cracker crust and bake about 40 minutes in a 350°F (180°C) oven.

Raspberry Topping: In a saucepan, combine the juice, cornstarch and SPLENDA® Granular. Stir until smooth and cook, stirring, until it begins to thicken. Stir in 1 package of raspberries and cook until the sauce is thick. Remove from heat and stir in the remaining raspberries. Pour over cheesecake and refrigerate overnight. **Serves 12.**

See photograph on page 35.

❖ BLUEBERRY SWIRL CHEESECAKE ❖

Unusual and very impressive.

Blueberry Purée:

1³/₄ cups	blueberries	425 mL
¹/₄ cup	SPLENDA® Granular	60 mL
4 tsp.	cornstarch	20 mL
4 tsp.	water	20 mL
2 tsp.	lemon juice	10 mL

Crust:

Crumb Crust, page 37, OR Sugarless
Sweet Dough Crust, page 45

Filling:

2 cups	low-fat ricotta cheese	500 mL
8 oz.	light cream cheese, softened	250 g
3	eggs	3
1 cup	skim milk yogurt	250 mL
1¹/₄ cups	SPLENDA® Granular	300 mL
2 tsp.	vanilla	10 mL
¹/₄ tsp.	salt	1 mL
¹/₂ cup	light sour cream	125 mL
¹/₄ cup	all-purpose flour	60 mL

Blueberry Purée: In a saucepan, combine all the purée ingredients, except lemon juice. Over medium heat, while stirring, heat the mixture until thickened. Place in a blender and purée with lemon juice. Cool.

Crust: Prepare crust as on page 37 or 45.

Filling: In a food processor or blender with a sharp blade, process the ricotta cheese until smooth. Add cream cheese and eggs. Beat until smooth. Add the remaining ingredients and beat until smooth. Pour the filling over the crust. Drop spoonfuls of the blueberry purée carefully over it. Using a knife, swirl lightly to create a marbled effect.

Prepare pan and bake as for Chocolate Swirl Cheesecake, page 41. **Serves 10-12.**

See photograph on page 35.

❖ STRAWBERRY CHEESECAKE ❖

It is difficult to believe this superb cheesecake is low-cal.

Crust:

| | Crumb Crust, page 37, OR Sugarless Sweet Dough Crust, page 45 | |

Filling:

2 cups	low-fat ricotta cheese	500 mL
8 oz.	light cream cheese, softened	250 g
3	eggs	3
1 cup	skim milk yogurt	250 mL
1 1/4 cups	SPLENDA® Granular	300 mL
1 tsp.	vanilla	5 mL
1/2 tsp.	salt	2 mL

Strawberry Topping:

3 tbsp.	cornstarch	45 mL
1/2 cup	reserved strawberry juice OR water	125 mL
3 cups	fresh OR frozen, unsweetened, sliced, thawed, drained strawberries	750 mL
1/2 cup	SPLENDA® Granular	125 mL
2	drops red food coloring (optional)	2

Crust: Prepare crust as on page 37 or 45.

Filling: In a food processor or blender with a sharp blade, process the ricotta cheese until smooth. Add the cream cheese and eggs. Beat. Add the yogurt, SPLENDA® Granular, vanilla and salt. Beat until very smooth. Pour the cream cheese mixture over the graham cracker crust and bake at 350°F (180°C) for 30-40 minutes, or until the center is set. Set aside to cool.

Strawberry Topping: Mix the cornstarch and juice or water in a saucepan. Add the fresh or thawed, sliced strawberries and SPLENDA® Granular. Over medium heat, cook until the sauce thickens and becomes translucent. Remove from the heat and add a couple of drops of red food coloring for a wonderful deep red color. Allow to cool. Spread the strawberry topping over the cooled cheesecake. **Serves 10-12.**

VARIATIONS: Substitute peaches or blueberries for the strawberries. Add 1 tbsp. (15 mL) lemon juice.

❖ FROSTED STRAWBERRY ❖
CHEESECAKE

Such a pretty dessert.

Vanilla Wafer Crust:

1¹/₃ cups	crushed vanilla wafers	325 mL
2 tbsp.	SPLENDA® Granular	30 mL
¹/₄ cup	diet margarine, melted	60 mL

Filling:

2 cups	low-fat ricotta cheese	500 mL
8 oz.	light cream cheese, softened	250 g
2	eggs	2
1 cup	skim milk yogurt	250 mL
1¹/₄ cups	SPLENDA® Granular	300 mL
¹/₄ cup	all-purpose flour	60 mL
2 tbsp.	orange juice	30 mL
1 tbsp.	finely grated orange peel	15 mL
2 drops	red food coloring (optional)	2 drops
1¹/₂ cups	hulled, sliced, fresh strawberries	375 mL
2 tbsp.	all-purpose flour	30 mL

Topping:

2 cups	commercial low-calorie whipped topping	500 mL
	fresh strawberries for garnish	

Crust: Combine all crust ingredients. Press into a greased 9" (23 cm) springform pan. Bake at 350°F (180°C) for 10 minutes. Cool. **OR**, use Sugarless Sweet Dough Crust, page 45.

Filling: In a blender or food processor with a sharp blade, process the ricotta cheese until smooth. Add cream cheese and eggs. Beat until smooth. Add yogurt, SPLENDA® Granular, flour, orange juice, grated orange peel and color. Purée strawberries and add to the cheesecake batter with the flour. Beat until smooth. Pour over the crust; bake at 350°F (180°C) for 35 minutes, or until set. Refrigerate overnight.

Topping: Prepare topping. Remove the cooled cheesecake from the pan. Spread the whipped topping over the cheesecake and garnish with fresh strawberries. (Make double the amount of topping if frosting the sides.) **Serves 10-12.**

See photograph on the front cover.

40

❖ CHOCOLATE SWIRL CHEESECAKE ❖

Chocolate swirls look and taste fabulous!

Chocolate Crumb Crust:

1¹/₃ cups	graham cracker crumbs	325 mL
¹/₄ cup	SPLENDA® Granular	60 mL
¹/₃ cup+1 tbsp.	diet margarine, melted	90 mL
2 tbsp.	cocoa	30 mL

Filling:

1¹/₂ cups	low-fat ricotta cheese	375 mL
8 oz.	light cream cheese, softened	250 g
¹/₂ cup	skim milk yogurt	125 mL
³/₄ cup	SPLENDA® Granular	175 mL
2 tbsp.	all-purpose flour	30 mL
1¹/₂ tsp.	vanilla	7 mL
3	egg whites	3
¹/₈ tsp.	salt	0.5 mL
3 tbsp.	SPLENDA® Granular	45 mL
3 tbsp.	unsweetened cocoa	45 mL
¹/₄ cup	SPLENDA® Granular	60 mL

Crust: Combine all crust ingredients. Press into a greased 9" (23 cm) springform pan. Bake at 350°F (180°C) for 10 minutes. Cool. **OR**, use Sugarless Chocolate Sweet Dough Crust, page 45.

Filling: In a blender or a food processor, with a sharp blade, process the ricotta cheese until very smooth. Add the cream cheese, yogurt and SPLENDA® Granular. Beat until well blended. Add the all-purpose flour and vanilla. Beat again. Transfer to a large mixing bowl.

Beat the egg whites and salt on medium speed until fairly firm. Gradually add 3 tbsp. (45 mL) SPLENDA® Granular and continue beating until stiff. Fold the egg whites into the cream cheese mixture in 2 batches. Set aside 1¹/₂ cups (375 mL) of the mixture. Pour the rest over the graham cracker crust.

Combine the cocoa and last amount of SPLENDA® Granular and gently fold into the reserved batter. Carefully place tablespoons of the cocoa mixture on top of the batter in the pan. Using a knife, swirl lightly to create a marbled effect.

Continued

Place the pan on a large sheet of foil. Wrap up the sides of the spring-form pan. Use another piece of foil and wrap up the remaining areas to make the springform pan waterproof. Place the springform pan in a large baking pan with boiling water that reaches 1" (2.5 cm) up the sides of the springform pan. Bake at 350°F (180°C) for approximately 30 minutes, or until just set. Switch the oven off and let the cheesecake stand in the oven for 1 hour. Remove the springform pan from the water bath and discard the foil. Time permitting, return cheesecake to the oven until completely cool. This even cooling will minimize cracking or eliminate it. Do not be concerned if the cheesecake has a couple of cracks, it will not detract from the appearance or taste. Cover and refrigerate. Serves 10-12.

❖ MARBLED BLACK FOREST CHEESECAKE ❖

This is my husband's favorite cheesecake.

Crust:

Chocolate Crumb Crust, page 41, OR
Sugarless Chocolate Sweet Dough
Crust, page 45

Filling:

2 cups	low-fat ricotta cheese	500 mL
8 oz.	light cream cheese, softened	250 g
1 cup	skim milk yogurt	250 mL
3	eggs	3
1¼ cups	SPLENDA® Granular	300 mL
½ x 14 oz.	can unsweetened cherries or cherries in light syrup, pitted and drained (reserve cherry juice)	½ x 398 mL
⅓ cup	whipping cream	75 mL
3 tbsp.	cocoa	45 mL
½ cup	SPLENDA® Granular	125 mL
2 tbsp.	all-purpose flour	30 mL

❖ MARBLED BLACK FOREST ❖ CHEESECAKE

Continued

Topping:

3 tbsp.	cornstarch	45 mL
³/₄ cup	reserved cherry juice OR water	175 mL
1¹/₂ x 14 oz.	cans unsweetened cherries or cherries in light syrup, pitted and drained	1¹/₂ x 398 mL
¹/₄ cup	SPLENDA® Granular	60 mL

Crust: Prepare the crust as on page 41 or 45, OR use reduced fat Chocolate Crumb Crust, see Helpful Hints, page 6.

Filling: In a food processor or blender with a sharp blade, process the ricotta cheese until smooth. Add cream cheese, yogurt, eggs and SPLENDA® Granular. Beat until smooth. Pour half the cheesecake filling over the baked crust. Arrange cherries on top of the batter.

Combine cream, cocoa, ¹/₂ cup (125 mL) SPLENDA® Granular and flour. Add to the reserved batter and beat until smooth. Pour over the cherries. Bake for 35 minutes at 350°F (180°C), or until the center is set.

Topping: In a saucepan, stir cornstarch into the reserved cherry juice or water. Add cherries and SPLENDA® Granular. Cook over medium heat until thickened. Cool slightly and pour over the cheesecake. Refrigerate at least 1 day before serving. **Serves 12.**

See photograph on the back cover.

Can we have our cake and eat it too?

A revealing comparison of a regular Marbled Black Forest Cheesecake versus the SPLENDA® Granular low-fat version:

	Total Calories	Calories per serving	Fat grams per serving
Regular Cheesecake	5400	450	27
SPLENDA® Granular Cheesecake	2304	192	10
Reduction in calories and fat:	3096	258	17

❖ DARK BLACK FOREST ❖
CHEESECAKE

Dark bittersweet chocolate layer — rich as can be.

Crust:

| | Chocolate Crumb Crust, page 41, OR Sugarless Chocolate Sweet Dough Crust, page 45 | |

Filling:

2 cups	low-fat ricotta cheese	500 mL
8 oz.	light cream cheese, softened	250 g
3	eggs	3
1 cup	skim milk yogurt	250 mL
1¹/₄ cups	SPLENDA® Granular	300 mL
¹/₂ x 14 oz.	can drained, pitted, cherries (reserve juice)	¹/₂ x 398 mL
3 oz.	unsweetened chocolate	85 g
¹/₃ cup	whipping cream	75 mL
¹/₂ cup	SPLENDA® Granular	125 mL

Topping:

3 tbsp.	cornstarch	45 mL
³/₄ cup	reserved cherry juice OR water	175 mL
1¹/₂ x 14-oz.	cans drained, pitted cherries	1¹/₂ x 398 mL
¹/₄ cup	SPLENDA® Granular	60 mL

Crust: Prepare crust as on page 41.

Filling: In a food processor or blender with a sharp blade, process the ricotta cheese until smooth. Add the cream cheese and eggs. Beat until smooth. Add the skim milk yogurt and SPLENDA® Granular. Beat again. Pour ¹/₂ the cheesecake filling over the baked crust. Arrange the cherries on top of the cheesecake batter.

Melt chocolate; stir in the whipping cream and SPLENDA® Granular. Add to reserved cheesecake batter and beat until smooth. Pour over cherries. Bake 35 minutes at 350°F (180°C), or until center sets.

Topping: In a saucepan, stir cornstarch into reserved juice or water. Add cherries and SPLENDA® Granular. Cook over medium heat until sauce thickens. Cool slightly and pour over cheesecake. The cheesecake tastes best after being refrigerated for 2 days. **Serves 10-12.**

❖ SINGLE CRUST FOR PIES ❖

A never-fail easy recipe.

1 cup	all-purpose flour	250 mL
1/4 tsp.	baking powder	1 mL
1/4 tsp.	salt	1 mL
1/4 cup	cold shortening	60 mL
1 tsp.	white vinegar	5 mL
3-5 tbsp.	ice water	45-75 mL

Sift the dry ingredients together. Using a pastry blender or your fingers, cut or rub in the shortening until the mixture resembles breadcrumbs. Using a fork to stir lightly, sprinkle the flour mixture with the combined vinegar and water, 1 tbsp. (15 mL) at a time, until the pastry holds together. Shape into a ball and flatten into a disk shape. Wrap in plastic and refrigerate overnight or for at least 1 hour.

Roll out pastry between 2 floured sheets of wax paper to an 11-12" (28-30 cm) circle. Line a 9" (23 cm) pie plate, trimming the sides neatly and fluting the edge. Prick crust all over with a fork to prevent lifting while baking. Bake at 400°F (200°C) for 15 minutes, or until lightly browned. Cool before filling. **Yield: pastry for 1, 9" (23 cm) pie.**

❖ SUGARLESS SWEET DOUGH CRUST ❖

My husband prefers this crust to traditional sweet crumb crusts.

1 cup	all-purpose flour	250 mL
1/4 tsp.	baking powder	1 mL
1/4 tsp.	salt	1 mL
1/3 cup	SPLENDA® Granular	75 mL
3 tbsp.	butter OR margarine	45 mL
2 tsp.	vanilla	10 mL
2	egg whites	2

Sift dry ingredients together. Rub in butter. Beat egg whites and vanilla until frothy. Stir into flour mixture with a fork. Add a little water if necessary. Roll dough on floured surface to fit a 9" (23 cm) springform pan or pie plate. Prick with fork. Bake at 350°F (180°C) for 15 minutes. Cool. **Yield: 1, 9" (23 cm) crust.**

VARIATION: For a **Sugarless Chocolate Sweet Dough Crust**, use 3/4 cup (175 mL) flour, 1/4 cup (60 mL) cocoa and 1/2 cup (125 mL) SPLENDA® Granular, plus the remaining ingredients above.

❖ VANILLA CREAM PIE ❖

A delicious basic and two variations.

Crust:

	Crumb Crust, page 37, OR Sugarless Sweet Dough Crust, page 45	

Filling:

1/3 cup	all-purpose flour	75 mL
1/2 cup	SPLENDA® Granular	125 mL
1/4 tsp.	salt	1 mL
2 1/4 cups	skim milk	550 mL
4	egg yolks	4
1 tbsp.	diet margarine	15 mL
1 tsp.	vanilla	5 mL

Topping:

2 cups	commercial low-calorie dessert topping OR Sugarless Whipped Topping, page 11	500 mL

Crust: Prepare crust as on pages 37 or 45.

Filling: In a saucepan, combine the flour, SPLENDA® Granular and salt. Pour the milk in gradually and stir with a wire whisk, over medium heat, until the mixture comes to a boil and thickens. Add some of the hot mixture to the egg yolks and beat slightly with the wire whisk. Return to the saucepan and cook over low heat for a few minutes, or until very thick. Do not boil. Remove from the heat.

Stir in the margarine and vanilla. Pour over the crust and cover with plastic wrap to prevent a skin from forming. Refrigerate.

Topping: Prepare topping. Spread over the surface of the cooled Vanilla Cream Pie. Keep refrigerated. **Serves 8.**

❖ BANANA CREAM PIE ❖

This pie may become one of your favorite recipes.

	ingredients for Vanilla Cream Pie, page 46	
3	medium bananas	3
1 tbsp.	lemon juice	15 mL

Prepare the crust, filling and topping as for Vanilla Cream Pie. Peel and slice the bananas and toss with the lemon juice. Place the bananas over the graham cracker crust. Allow the filling to cool slightly before pouring over the bananas. Spread whipped topping overall. If desired, garnish with banana slices dipped in lemon juice to prevent discoloration. Keep refrigerated. **Serves 8.**

See photograph on the back cover.

❖ LEMON CREAM PIE ❖

Smooth and creamy with a delightful lemony flavor.

	ingredients for Vanilla Cream Pie, page 46, except increase SPLENDA® Granular to $^2/_3$ cup (150 mL) and decrease skim milk to $1^3/_4$ cups (425 mL) omit the vanilla and stir in	
$^1/_4$ cup	lemon juice	60 mL
1 tsp.	grated lemon peel	5 mL

Follow the method for the Vanilla Cream Pie. **Serves 8.**

❖ CHOCOLATE CREAM PIE ❖

This gooey, rich pie will satisfy a craving for chocolate anyday!

Crust:

Chocolate Crumb Crust, page 41, OR
Sugarless Chocolate Sweet Dough Crust,
page 45

Filling:

1/3 cup+2 tbsp.	all-purpose flour	105 mL
1/4 cup	cocoa	60 mL
1 1/4 cups	SPLENDA® Granular	300 mL
1/4 tsp.	salt	1 mL
1 3/4 cups	skim milk	425 mL
1 oz.	unsweetened chocolate, melted	30 g
3	egg yolks	3
1 tsp.	diet margarine	5 mL
1 tbsp.	chocolate syrup (optional)	15 mL

Topping:

2 cups	commercial low-calorie dessert topping OR Sugarless Whipped Topping, page 11	500 mL

Crust: Prepare crust as on page 41 or 45.

Filling: In a saucepan, combine the flour, cocoa, SPLENDA® Granular and salt. Stir the milk in gradually and whisk until smooth. Stir the chocolate into the milk mixture. Stir with a wire whisk, over medium heat, until it boils and becomes thick. Add some of the hot chocolate mixture to the egg yolks and beat slightly with the wire whisk. Return to the saucepan and cook over low heat until very thick. Do not boil. Remove from the heat and stir in the margarine and chocolate syrup. Immediately pour over the graham cracker crust and cover with plastic wrap to prevent a skin from forming. Refrigerate.

Topping: Prepare the topping. Spread over the cooled pie. Keep refrigerated. **Serves 8.**

❖ MILK TART ❖

An old-fashioned custard tart or pie popular in many countries.

Crust:

1/2 cup	self-raising cake and pastry flour	125 mL
1/8 tsp.	salt	0.5 mL
1 tbsp.	SPLENDA® Granular	15 mL
1 tbsp.	cold shortening	15 mL
1	large egg	1

Filling:

2 cups	skim milk	500 mL
1	cinnamon stick	1
3 tbsp.	all-purpose flour	45 mL
1/4 cup	SPLENDA® Granular	60 mL
1 tbsp.	cornstarch	15 mL
1/4 tsp.	salt	1 mL
2 tbsp.	margarine	30 mL
3	eggs, beaten	3
	cinnamon and SPLENDA® Granular	

Crust: Combine the flour, salt and SPLENDA® Granular. Rub in the shortening until the mixture resembles breadcrumbs. Beat the egg and stir it in with a fork. Knead lightly and roll the dough very thinly between 2 floured pieces of wax paper. Line an 8" (20 cm) pie plate on the bottom and sides. Trim.

Filling: Put the skim milk and cinnamon stick in a saucepan. Scald the milk. Remove the cinnamon stick. Combine the dry ingredients. Add a little hot milk to the dry ingredients, stirring until smooth. Return this mixture to the saucepan; cook and stir on low-medium heat until thickened. Remove from the heat and add the margarine. Cool a little while. Fold in the well-beaten eggs and pour over the piecrust.

Bake at 375°F (190°C) for approximately 10 minutes. Reduce the heat to 350°F (180°C) and bake a further 10 minutes. Cool slightly and sprinkle lightly with a cinnamon-SPLENDA® Granular mixture.
Serves 8.

❖ To scald means to heat to just below the boiling point.

❖ CUSTARD PIE ❖

Creamy, pudding-like filling.

Crust:

1¹/4 cups	all-purpose flour	300 mL
¹/4 cup	SPLENDA® Granular	60 mL
1 tsp.	baking powder	5 mL
¹/4 tsp.	salt	1 mL
3 tbsp.	cold shortening	45 mL
2	egg yolks, slightly beaten	2
6-8 tbsp.	cold water	90-120 mL

Filling:

¹/2 cup	SPLENDA® Granular	125 mL
¹/4 tsp.	salt	1 mL
6 tbsp.	custard powder	90 mL
1¹/2 cups	skim milk	375 mL
¹/2 tsp.	vanilla	2 mL
1 tbsp.	diet margarine	15 mL
2	egg whites, stiffly beaten, OR 2 cups (500 mL) Sugarless Whipped Topping, page 11, OR alternative, page 64	2

Crust: Combine the dry ingredients and rub in the shortening. Add the beaten egg yolks and stir lightly with a fork. Add the cold water, 1 tbsp. (15 mL) at a time, mixing lightly with a fork. Press the dough over the bottom and completely up the sides of a 9" (23 cm) pie plate. Pierce the crust all over with a fork. Set aside a small piece of dough and bake separately. Pinch the edges for an attractive finish. Bake at 350°F (180°C) for 15-20 minutes until slightly browned.

Filling: Combine dry ingredients and stir in a little skim milk, until smooth. Set aside. Boil the remaining milk in a saucepan and stir in the custard mixture. Cook over low heat, stirring constantly with a wire whisk, until thickened. Remove from the heat and stir in the vanilla and margarine. If the custard is a little lumpy, blend in a food processor until completely smooth. Fold in the stiffly beaten egg whites or 2 cups (500 mL) of the Sugarless Whipped Topping, page 11.

Pour the filling over the cooled crust. Crush the extra piece of baked crust and sprinkle the crumbs over the custard pie. Cover and chill thoroughly before serving. **Serves 8.**

❖ GLAZED BLUEBERRY CHEESE PIE ❖

A very showy pie — excellent!

1	single baked piecrust, page 45	1

Filling:

1 cup	low-fat cottage cheese	250 mL
4 oz.	light cream cheese, softened	115 g
1/2 cup	SPLENDA® Granular	125 mL
1 tbsp.	lemon juice	15 mL

Blueberry Topping:

3 tbsp.	cornstarch	45 mL
1/2 cup	reserved blueberry juice OR water	125 mL
3 cups	fresh OR frozen, unsweetened, thawed, drained blueberries	750 mL
1/2 cup	SPLENDA® Granular	125 mL

Prepare the piecrust and bake as directed on page 45. Cool.

Filling: In a blender or a food processor, using a sharp blade, beat the cottage cheese until it is very smooth. Add the cream cheese, SPLENDA® Granular and lemon juice. Beat again until smooth. Fill the cooled piecrust and chill.

Blueberry Topping: Place the cornstarch in a saucepan and gradually stir in the juice or water until smooth. Add the blueberries. Stirring constantly, over medium heat, cook until the mixture thickens. Add SPLENDA® Granular, stirring well. Allow to cool slightly.

Pour topping over the chilled cheese layer and refrigerate the pie.
Serves 8.

VARIATION: Glazed Strawberry Cheese Pie — Substitute 3 cups (750 mL) fresh or frozen, unsweetened, thawed and drained strawberries for the blueberries.

❖ PINEAPPLE CHEESE PIE ❖

A winner for pineapple lovers.

1	unbaked single piecrust, page 45	1

Filling:

14 oz.	can unsweetened, crushed pineapple, with juice	398 mL
2 tbsp.	cornstarch	30 mL
1/3 cup	SPLENDA® Granular	75 mL
1 1/2 cups	low-fat ricotta cheese	375 mL
4 oz.	light cream cheese, softened	115 g
1 tsp.	vanilla	5 mL
2/3 cup	SPLENDA® Granular	150 mL
1/4 tsp.	salt	1 mL
1	egg	1

Topping:

2 cups	commercial low-calorie dessert topping OR Sugarless Whipped Topping, page 11	500 mL
	sliced, blanched almonds (optional)	

Prepare the piecrust, page 45. Do not bake.

Filling: In a saucepan, while stirring, bring the pineapple, juice and cornstarch to a boil. Stir in the first amount of SPLENDA® Granular. Set aside. In a blender or food processor with a sharp blade, on high speed, cream the ricotta cheese until very smooth. Add the cream cheese. Blend. Add the vanilla, second amount of SPLENDA® Granular, salt and egg. Beat very well once again.

Spread the pineapple mixture over the unbaked piecrust. Pour the cheese mixture evenly overall and bake at 350°F (180°C) for approximately 25 minutes, or until set and browning slightly in places. Cool thoroughly and refrigerate.

Topping: Prepare the topping. Spread over the cooled pie. Sprinkle with sliced, blanched almonds, if desired. Refrigerate the pie. **Serves 8.**

VARIATION: Peach Cheese Pie — Substitute a 20 oz. (600 g) package of frozen, unsweetened peaches and juice for pineapple and juice. Also substitute quick-cooking tapioca for cornstarch and increase SPLENDA® Granular to 3/4 cup (175 mL).

Apple Lattice Pie, page 59
Bumbleberry Tart, page 57

❖ STRAWBERRY RHUBARB PIE ❖

This double-crust pie is my dad's favorite pie.

Double Crust:

2 1/4 cups	cake and pastry flour	550 mL
3/4 tsp.	salt	3 mL
1/2 tbsp.	SPLENDA® Granular	7 mL
2/3 cup	cold shortening	150 mL
6-8 tbsp.	ice water	90-120 mL

Filling:

3 tbsp.	all-purpose flour	45 mL
1 cup	SPLENDA® Granular	250 mL
1	egg, well-beaten	1
3 cups	chopped rhubarb, 1" (2.5 cm) pieces	750 mL
1 cup	hulled, sliced strawberries	250 mL
1 tbsp.	SPLENDA® Granular	15 mL

Topping:

1/2 tsp.	SPLENDA® Granular	2 mL
	frozen low-calorie whipped topping OR	
	Sugarless Whipped topping, page 11	

Crust: Sift the dry ingredients together. Rub in the shortening. Add the ice water gradually, stirring lightly with a fork, until the pastry holds together. Shape into 2 balls, 1 slightly larger than the other. Roll the larger ball to fit a 9" (23 cm) pie dish, leaving a small overhang. Roll the smaller ball to fit over the filling.

Filling: Combine the flour and 1 cup (250 mL) SPLENDA® Granular with the beaten egg. Add the rhubarb and strawberries. Stir well. Turn into the piecrust. Sprinkle the fruit with 1 tbsp. (15 mL) SPLENDA® Granular.

Moisten the edges of the bottom pastry and fit the smaller rolled pastry over the top. Trim and crimp to seal. Cut about 5 large slits in the top crust, to allow steam to escape.

Place the pie dish on a shallow metal baking pan to catch spills. Bake at 350°F (180°C) for approximately 50 minutes, or until slightly browned.

Topping: Sprinkle the piecrust with 1/2 tsp. (2 mL) SPLENDA® Granular. Serve with whipped topping, if desired. **Serves 8.**

❖ STRAWBERRY PIE ❖

This eye-catching pie is great; enjoy it even during midwinter.

1	baked single piecrust, page 45	1
Filling:		
1 cup	reserved strawberry juice OR water (for fresh strawberries)	250 mL
2 tbsp.	cornstarch	30 mL
1/8 tsp.	salt	0.5 mL
3/4 cup	SPLENDA® Granular	175 mL
4 cups	fresh OR frozen, unsweetened, thawed, drained strawberries	1 L
Topping:		
2 cups	commercial low-calorie dessert topping OR Sugarless Whipped Topping, page 11	500 mL

Prepare the piecrust as directed on page 45.

Filling: In a saucepan, gradually add the strawberry juice/water mixture or water to the cornstarch and stir until smooth. Continue stirring and bring to the boil over medium heat. Stir in the salt and SPLENDA® Granular. Allow to cool slightly and fold in the strawberries.

Fill the baked piecrust with the strawberry mixture and chill.

Topping: Prepare the topping. Layer the prepared whipped topping carefully over the chilled pie. **Serves 8.**

VARIATION: Blueberry Pie — Substitute 4 cups (1 L) fresh or frozen, unsweetened, thawed, drained blueberries for the strawberries. Add 2 tsp. (10 mL) grated lemon rind.

❖ BUMBLEBERRY TART ❖

Raspberries and blueberries are a superb visual and flavor combination.

1	unbaked single piecrust, page 45	1
Filling:		
1/4 cup	all-purpose flour	60 mL
2/3 cup	SPLENDA® Granular	150 mL
1/8 tsp.	salt	0.5 mL
1/4 tsp.	cinnamon	1 mL
3 cups	fresh OR frozen, unsweetened, thawed, drained raspberries	750 mL
3 cups	fresh OR frozen, unsweetened, thawed, drained blueberries	750 mL
Topping:		
	frozen low-calorie whipped topping OR Sugarless Whipped Topping, page 11	

Prepare the piecrust according to recipe on page 45, but do not bake.

Filling: Mix the flour, SPLENDA® Granular, salt and cinnamon together. Sprinkle half this mixture over the pastry shell. Set aside 1/2 cup (125 mL) raspberries for garnishing the top of the tart later. Top with 1/2 the fruit, the rest of the flour mixture, and the remaining fruit.

Bake in a 400°F (200°C) oven on the lowest rack for about 30-40 minutes, or until the fruit is bubbly and the crust is slightly browned.

Topping: Allow pie to cool and garnish with the reserved raspberries. Serve cold with a dollop of low-calorie whipped topping. This pie is wonderful served with low-calorie vanilla ice cream. **Serves 8.**

See photograph on page 53.

❖ BLUEBERRY/STRAWBERRY FLAN ❖

Often on the menu in the best hotels, except this is low-cal.

Sponge Flan:

1¹/₄ cups	cake and pastry flour	300 mL
1¹/₂ tsp.	baking powder	7 mL
¹/₄ tsp.	salt	1 mL
¹/₂ cup	SPLENDA® Granular	125 mL
¹/₃ cup	butter OR margarine, softened	75 mL
2	eggs	2
1 tsp.	vanilla	5 mL
¹/₃ cup	skim milk	75 mL

Pastry Cream:

¹/₄ cup	sifted all-purpose flour	60 mL
¹/₈ tsp.	salt	0.5 mL
¹/₃ cup	SPLENDA® Granular	75 mL
1¹/₂ cups	skim milk	375 mL
1	egg, slightly beaten	1
1 tsp.	vanilla	5 mL

Filling:

¹/₃ oz.	sugarless, artificially sweetened, strawberry jelly powder	11 g
10	large, fresh strawberries	10
2 cups	fresh blueberries	500 mL

Sponge Flan: Sift dry ingredients together. Beat the butter for 1 minute. Add eggs and vanilla. Beat again. To egg mixture, add dry ingredients and skim milk simultaneously in 3 additions, beating well after each addition, until smooth. Pour into a greased 8" (20 cm) flan pan. Bake for 15-20 minutes and turn out on a cake rack to cool.

Pastry Cream: Combine flour, salt and SPLENDA® Granular in a saucepan and, over medium heat, gradually add the milk using a wire whisk. Cook until boiling. Add a little of this hot mixture to the beaten egg and return it to the saucepan. Over low heat, cook for 2 minutes. Do not boil. Remove from heat and stir in the vanilla. Pour into a small bowl and cover with plastic wrap to prevent a skin from forming. Chill.

Filling: In a small saucepan over low heat, dissolve half the jelly powder in a little water. Brush over flan; let set for a few minutes. Spread pastry cream over flan. Decorate with berries. If desired, dissolve remaining jelly in water; brush over the fruit to glaze. **Serves 6-8.**

❖ APPLE LATTICE PIE ❖

My sons ask for 2 of these apple pies instead of birthday cake!!!

Cookie Crust:

2 cups	all-purpose flour	500 mL
1/2 cup	SPLENDA® Granular	125 mL
1/8 tsp.	salt	0.5 mL
2/3 cup	cold shortening	150 mL
2	large egg yolks	2
1/2 cup	ice cold water	125 mL
1/2 tsp.	vanilla	2 mL

Filling:

2/3 cup	SPLENDA® Granular	150 mL
2 tbsp.	all-purpose flour	30 mL
1/2 tsp.	ground cinnamon	2 mL
1/8 tsp.	ground nutmeg	0.5 mL
7-8 cups	peeled, thinly sliced apples	1.75-2 L
1/4 cup	orange juice OR lemon juice	60 mL
1 tbsp.	diet margarine	15 mL

Cookie Crust: Combine the flour, SPLENDA® Granular and salt in a large bowl. Cut in the shortening until the mixture is crumbly in texture. Beat the egg yolks, water and vanilla. Sprinkle onto the flour mixture, a little at a time, stirring lightly with a fork until the pastry holds together. Knead lightly, then shape the pastry into 2 balls, 1 a little larger than the other. Flatten the balls, wrap and refrigerate 1 hour. Roll between 2 floured pieces of wax paper. Roll the larger ball into a 11-12" (28-30 cm) circle and the other into a 9-10" (23-25 cm) circle. Line a deep 9" (23 cm) pie dish with the larger circle and trim the edges.

Filling: Combine SPLENDA® Granular with flour, cinnamon and nutmeg. Toss the sliced apples with orange juice. Place half the apples in piecrust and sprinkle with half the cinnamon mixture. Repeat. Dot apple filling with margarine. With a fluted pastry cutter or knife, cut 1/2" (1.3 cm) wide strips out of the remaining pastry circle (or use a lattice pastry cutter). Weave the strips over the filling in a lattice pattern. Bake at 375°F (190°C) for approximately 45 minutes, or until the apples are soft. If the pie is already browning well, but the apples are still not soft, cover with pierced foil. **Serves 8.**

See photograph on page 53.

❖ PEACH LATTICE PIE ❖
Superb fresh peach flavor.

Crust:		
1	Cookie Crust, page 59	1

Filling:		
5^1/$_2$ cups	peeled, sliced, firm, fresh peaches	1.375 L
1^1/$_4$ cups	SPLENDA® Granular	300 mL
3 tbsp.	quick-cooking tapioca	45 mL
^{1}/$_4$ tsp.	cinnamon	1 mL

Crust: Prepare the Cookie Crust on page 59.

Filling: Combine the peaches, SPLENDA® Granular, tapioca and cinnamon, mixing well. Fill the prepared pastry shell. Roll the remaining pastry ball to fit over the top of the pie. With a fluted pastry cutter or knife, cut ^{1}/$_2$" (1.3 cm) wide strips (or use a lattice pastry cutter). Weave the strips over the filling in a lattice pattern.

Place the pie on a shallow metal baking pan to catch spills. Bake at 400°F (200°C) for 30 minutes, then reduce the heat to 375°F (190°C). Bake a further 15 minutes, or until the filling is bubbling and the crust is slightly browned. During baking, if the crust is browning too quickly, cover pie loosely with foil. **Serves 8.**

VARIATION: Cherry Lattice Pie — Substitute 5^1/$_2$ cups (1.375 L) pitted, fresh, tart cherries for the peaches and 3 tbsp. (45 mL) cornstarch for the quick-cooking tapioca. Omit the cinnamon. Dot the fruit with 1 tbsp. (15 mL) diet margarine.

❖ If preferred, use the double crust pastry recipe as for the Strawberry Rhubarb Pie, page 55.

❖ FRUIT PIZZA ❖

A spectacular dessert! It looks like food art.

Crust:

1¹/₄ cups	all-purpose flour	300 mL
¹/₄ cup	SPLENDA® Granular	60 mL
¹/₂ cup	margarine	125 mL

Filling:

1¹/₂ cups	low-fat cottage cheese	375 mL
4 oz .	light cream cheese, softened	115 g
1 tsp.	vanilla	5 mL
¹/₃ cup	SPLENDA® Granular	75 mL

Topping:

fresh OR canned fruit of your choice
(strawberries, peaches, blueberries,
raspberries, blackberries, pineapple,
kiwi fruit, mandarin oranges, grapes etc.)

Glaze:

1 cup	unsweetened pineapple juice	250 mL
2 tbsp.	cornstarch	30 mL
1 tsp.	lemon juice	5 mL
¹/₂ cup	SPLENDA® Granular	125 mL

Crust: Combine the flour and SPLENDA® Granular. Rub in the margarine and press into a greased 12" (30 cm) pizza pan. Bake at 350°F (180°C) for 8-10 minutes.

Filling: In a blender or food processor with a sharp blade, cream the cottage cheese until completely smooth. Add the cream cheese, vanilla and SPLENDA® Granular. Beat again. Smooth this mixture over the cooled crust.

Topping: Place fruit on the cheese layer in an attractive design.

Glaze: In a saucepan, over medium heat, combine the pineapple juice, cornstarch, lemon juice and SPLENDA® Granular. Bring to a boil and cook slightly longer until the glaze is translucent. If the glaze is too thick, thin with a little water. Pour glaze over fruit or brush on with a pastry brush. The glaze must cover the whole fruit pizza. Refrigerate. **Serves 10-12.**

See photograph on the back cover.

❖ SPICED DATE PUDDING WITH ❖ LEMON SAUCE

An unusual and delicious pudding.

Pudding:

2 cups	fresh breadcrumbs	500 mL
1 cup	skim milk	250 mL
2 tbsp.	diet margarine	30 mL
1 cup	all-purpose flour	250 mL
1/2 cup	SPLENDA® Granular	125 mL
1 tsp.	salt	5 mL
1/2 tsp.	cinnamon	2 mL
1/4 tsp.	allspice	1 mL
1/2 tsp.	ground ginger	2 mL
1/2 tsp.	baking soda	2 mL
4 oz.	dates	115 g

Lemon Sauce:

1/2 cup	SPLENDA® Granular	125 mL
1 tbsp.	cornstarch	15 mL
1 cup	boiling water	250 mL
1 tbsp.	diet margarine	15 mL
2 tbsp.	lemon juice	30 mL
1 tsp.	grated lemon rind	5 mL
1/8 tsp.	salt	0.5 mL

Pudding: Soak the breadcrumbs in the milk. Melt the margarine and pour over the breadcrumb mixture.

Sift the dry ingredients together and stir into the breadcrumb mixture. Cut the dates into small pieces and fold in. Turn the pudding into a greased 8" (20 cm) pie plate. Bake in a 350°F (180°C) oven for 25-30 minutes.

Lemon Sauce: Combine SPLENDA® Granular and cornstarch. Add the boiling water gradually, stirring all the time. Boil 3 minutes. Remove from the heat and add the margarine, lemon juice, lemon rind and salt. Stir until the margarine has melted. Serve hot over the Date Pudding. **Serves 4-6.**

❖ SNOW PUDDING ❖

Chiffon-light.

1 tbsp.	gelatin (1 env.)	15 mL
1/4 cup	cold water	60 mL
1 cup	boiling water	250 mL
3/4 cup	SPLENDA® Granular	175 mL
1/4 cup	lemon juice	60 mL
2 tsp.	grated lemon rind	10 mL
2	egg whites OR 1 1/4 cups (300 mL)	2
	Sugarless Whipped Topping, page 11	

Soak the gelatin in the cold water, then dissolve it in the boiling water. Stir in SPLENDA® Granular, lemon juice and grated lemon rind. Chill the mixture until almost set.

Beat the egg whites until stiff peaks form. When the gelatin mixture begins to set, beat until light and spongy, about 30 seconds. Fold the egg whites or Sugarless Whipped Topping into the gelatin mixture. Pour into a 4-cup (1 L) pudding mold. Serve with Custard Sauce, page 81. **Serves 4.**

❖ ORANGE JELLY ❖

Cool and light for a hot day.

2 tbsp.	gelatin (2 env.)	30 mL
2 tbsp.	cold water	30 mL
1 cup	boiling water	250 mL
1/2 cup	SPLENDA® Granular	125 mL
1 cup	orange juice	250 mL
1 cup	cold water	250 mL
10 oz.	can mandarin oranges, drained (optional)	284 mL

Add the gelatin to cold water. Stir, then dissolve it in the boiling water. Add SPLENDA® Granular, stirring well. Stir in the orange juice and cold water. Allow to set. If desired, just as the jelly begins to set, fold in 1 cup (250 mL) drained, canned mandarin oranges.

Serve with Custard Sauce, page 81, if desired. Any fruit juice and fruit can be substituted. For another variation, omit the cold water and substitute 1 cup (250 mL) cold, creamy milk. **Serves 4.**

❖ BANANA CITRUS MOUSSE ❖

A light and lovely fruit dessert.

1¹/₂ tbsp.	gelatin	22 mL
¹/₄ cup	cold water	60 mL
¹/₄ cup	boiling water	60 mL
2	oranges	2
4	bananas, mashed	4
1 tbsp.	lemon juice	15 mL
²/₃ cup	SPLENDA® Granular	150 mL
1 tsp.	vanilla	5 mL
1 cup	commercial low-calorie dessert topping OR Sugarless Whipped Topping, page 11	250 mL

Soak the gelatin in the cold water, then dissolve in the boiling water. Squeeze the juice out of the oranges or use a juice extractor. Stir the orange juice into the mashed bananas and lemon juice.

Add SPLENDA® Granular, the vanilla and the dissolved gelatin. Mix well. Chill.

When the gelatin dessert just begins to set, fold in the prepared whipped topping or Sugarless Whipped Topping. Pour into a pudding mold and refrigerate until set. **Serves 4.**

❖ If using the Sugarless Whipped Topping, use the remainder for garnish when serving.

❖ CHOCOLATE BANANA MOUSSE ❖

A very popular creamy combination of flavors.

1 tbsp.	unflavored gelatin (1 env.)	15 mL
1/4 cup	cold water	60 mL
2 cups	mashed bananas	500 mL
1 tsp.	vanilla	5 mL
4 tsp.	cocoa powder	20 mL
1/2 cup	SPLENDA® Granular	125 mL
1/2 cup	light sour cream OR plain yogurt	125 mL
2	egg whites OR alternatives below	2
1/4 tsp.	cream of tartar	1 mL

Stir the gelatin into the cold water and dissolve it over low heat.

Blend the mashed bananas and vanilla until smooth. Add the cocoa powder, SPLENDA® Granular, gelatin mixture and the sour cream. Blend at high speed until smooth. Refrigerate until slightly thickened.

Make sure the egg whites are at room temperature. On high speed, beat until frothy for approximately 30 seconds. Add the cream of tartar and beat at high speed for another 2 minutes, or until stiff peaks form.

Fold into the chilled mousse and refrigerate in 4 separate dessert bowls to set. **Serves 4.**

VARIATION: **Strawberry Banana Mousse** — Substitute 1 cup (250 mL) of mashed bananas and 1 cup (250 mL) strawberries for the 2 cups (500 mL) of bananas used above. Omit cocoa powder.

❖ If you are concerned about the risk of salmonella associated with the use of raw egg whites, the following produces wonderful results. Fold 2 cups (500 mL) Sugarless Whipped Topping, page 11, into the chilled mousse. Use the leftover whipped topping for garnish (recipe makes 3 cups [750 mL]). OR, use half a 4.4 oz. (125 g) package (4 tbsp. [60 mL]) of meringue dessert mix (egg white powder) plus 1/4 cup (60 mL) of lukewarm water. Gradually stir the water into the powder mixture. Stir approximately 15 seconds. Beat with electric mixer at the highest speed for about 4 minutes, or until very thick. Fold into the chilled mousse and refrigerate as mentioned above.

❖ CHOCOLATE STRAWBERRY ❖ CREAM CUPS

This candy dessert looks very elegant.

Chocolate Cups:

1 cup	commercial low-calorie dessert topping	250 mL
6 oz.	unsweetened chocolate squares	170 g
2 tbsp.	margarine, not diet	30 mL
1¼ cups	SPLENDA® Granular	300 mL
4-5 tbsp.	chocolate syrup, OR less to taste	60-75 mL

Filling:

2 cups	fresh OR frozen, unsweetened, thawed, drained strawberries, reserving 5 for garnish	500 mL
2 cups	commercial low-calorie dessert topping	500 mL
1 tsp.	cornstarch	5 mL
¼ cup	SPLENDA® Granular	60 mL

Chocolate Cups: Prepare the whipped topping according to the manufacturer's instructions. Microwave the chocolate on high for 3 minutes, or until melted. Stir in the whipped topping, margarine, SPLENDA® Granular and chocolate syrup to taste.

Place 10 small paper cups in a muffin pan. Allow the chocolate to cool slightly. Put 3 heaped tsp. (20 mL) in a paper cup and use the back of the spoon to spread it evenly over the bottom and up the sides. Repeat 9 times. Refrigerate cups until hardened. Remove the papers and fill chocolate cups.

Filling: Use fresh or frozen, unsweetened, thawed and drained strawberries, reserving 5 of the nicest for garnish. Slice thinly. Prepare the topping beating in cornstarch and SPLENDA® Granular. Fold in the sliced strawberries.

Garnish the top of each Chocolate Strawberry Cream Cup with a strawberry half. Keep refrigerated. **Yield: 10.**

See photograph on the back cover.

❖ CHOCOLATE COCOA CREAM CUPS ❖

A variation of the Chocolate Strawberry Cream Cups. Great.

10	chocolate cups, page 66	10
Filling:		
2 cups	commercial low-calorie dessert topping	500 mL
1 tsp.	cornstarch	5 mL
1/4 cup	SPLENDA® Granular	60 mL
2 tbsp.	cocoa	30 mL
1/4 tsp.	vanilla	1 mL
1 oz.	chocolate shavings for garnish (optional)	30 g

Filling: Prepare the whipped topping, and beat in the cornstarch, SPLENDA® Granular, cocoa and the vanilla. Fill the chocolate cups. Garnish with chocolate shavings, if desired. **Yield: 10.**

❖ CHOCOLATE ORANGE ❖ CREAM CUPS

This variation tastes similar to a liqueur chocolate treat.

10	chocolate cups, page 66	10
Filling:		
2 cups	commercial low-calorie dessert topping	500 mL
1 tsp.	cornstarch	5 mL
1/4 cup	SPLENDA® Granular	60 mL
1/2 tsp.	orange extract	2 mL
4 drops	yellow food coloring	4 drops
2 drops	red food coloring	2 drops
	fresh orange slices OR canned mandarin orange segments, drained, for garnish	

Filling: Prepare the whipped topping, and beat in the next 5 ingredients. Fill the chocolate cups and garnish with orange slices or mandarin orange segments. **Yield: 10.**

❖ VANILLA ICE CREAM ❖

Rich and creamy. Be sure to try the marvelous variations.

2 cups	1% milk	500 mL
1³/₄ cups	whole milk	425 mL
1 cup	whipping cream	250 mL
3 cups	2% evaporated milk	750 mL
¹/₂ tsp.	salt	2 mL
1³/₄ cups	SPLENDA® Granular	425 mL
4 tsp.	vanilla	20 mL

An ice cream and yogurt maker is required. Combine all the ingredients in the ice cream can. Follow the manufacturer's instructions. If you do not have a machine, use the alternative method on page 70.
Yield: 4 quarts (4 L).

VARIATIONS: Banana Ice Cream — Add 3¹/₂ cups (875 mL) mashed, ripe bananas before freezing.

Peach Ice Cream — Add 4 cups (1 L) puréed peaches before freezing.

Strawberry Ice Cream — Add 4 cups (1 L) puréed strawberries before freezing.

❖ Alternative substitute ingredients are given on page 70, for even richer, creamier recipes, but the calories will be higher.

❖ CHOCOLATE ICE CREAM ❖

This ice cream is a family favorite.

1 tbsp.	cornstarch	15 mL
2 tbsp.	cocoa	30 mL
¹/₂ tsp.	salt	2 mL
1¹/₂ cups	SPLENDA® Granular	375 mL
2 cups	skim milk	500 mL
1 cup	whole milk	250 mL
2	egg yolks	2
1 oz.	unsweetened chocolate, melted	30 g
1 cup	whipping cream	250 mL
¹/₂ cup	whole milk	125 mL
1 tsp.	vanilla	5 mL

❖ CHOCOLATE ICE CREAM ❖

Continued

Combine the cornstarch, cocoa, salt and SPLENDA® Granular in a saucepan. Gradually add the skim milk and 1 cup (250 mL) whole milk. Stir constantly over medium heat until the mixture begins to simmer. Stir ¾ cup (175 mL) of the hot mixture into the egg yolks and return to the saucepan. Cook over very low heat for 3 minutes, stirring constantly.

Remove from the heat and whisk in the chocolate until smooth. Pour into the ice cream can and add the whipping cream, whole milk and vanilla. Stir well. Cover and refrigerate for 2 hours. Follow the manufacturer's instructions for freezing. **Yield: 2 quarts (2 L).**

❖ SUMMER FRUIT SORBETS ❖

A refreshing, light treat.

⅔ cup	**water**	150 mL
⅓ cup	**SPLENDA® Granular**	75 mL
1½ cups	**frozen, unsweetened strawberries**	375 mL

Bring the water and SPLENDA® Granular to a boil in a saucepan. Simmer a few minutes. Allow to cool and refrigerate at least 2 hours.

Defrost the strawberries until just softening a little. Place the strawberries and SPLENDA® Granular mixture in a blender and process until smooth. Freeze for 30 minutes, or until ready to serve. **Serves 2.**

VARIATIONS: Make this wonderful low-cal dessert with frozen, unsweetened peaches, raspberries, etc. Use your imagination.

❖ An ice cream machine is a worthwhile investment for these exciting ice cream and frozen yogurt recipes. The result is always an unbeatable smooth, creamy texture. It is difficult to prevent ice crystals from forming with the manual method.

❖ Ice creams and frozen yogurts taste their creamiest when freshly made or when frozen for a short while. Ice creams and frozen yogurts stored in your freezer will freeze solid, but microwaving a couple of minutes corrects that quickly.

❖ FROZEN STRAWBERRY YOGURT ❖

Creamy and rich tasting.

3 cups	fresh OR frozen, unsweetened, thawed, sliced, strawberries	750 mL
4 cups	plain yogurt	1 L
4 cups	skim milk yogurt	1 L
2 cups	2% evaporated milk*	500 mL
1¾ cups	SPLENDA® Granular	425 mL

With an inexpensive ice cream and frozen yogurt maker, this recipe is as simple as combining all the ingredients in the ice cream can and mixing well. The ice cream maker does the work. Follow the manufacturer's instructions for making and hardening the ice cream. **Yield: 4 quarts.**

Alternatively, freeze in your home freezer in a large plastic container, remembering to leave ½" (1.3 cm) for expansion. Stir several times during the freezing process. For a smoother texture, remove the partially frozen ice cream and process in a blender or food processor. Stir in the fruit at this stage. Freeze again, stirring occasionally.

* For a creamier texture and richer flavor, replace evaporated milk with whipping cream if you don't mind the calories.

❖ FROZEN BLUEBERRY YOGURT ❖

Wonderful fruit flavor!

5 cups	fresh OR frozen, unsweetened, thawed blueberries	1.25 L
2½ cups	plain yogurt	625 mL
2½ cups	skim milk yogurt	625 mL
2 cups	whole milk	500 mL
2 cups	SPLENDA® Granular	500 mL

An ice cream and yogurt maker is required. Mash the blueberries before combining with the rest of the ingredients in the ice cream can. Mix well. Follow the manufacturer's directions, or use the alternative freezing method above. **Yield: 4 quarts.**

❖ Some alternative ingredients to use in the frozen yogurt and ice cream recipes for even richer results: Substitute whole milk for 1% milk, half and half for whole milk, whipping cream for 2% evaporated milk and plain yogurt for skim milk yogurt. The calories will be much higher, but these guidelines leave room for some experimentation.

Black Forest Cake, page 29

❖ OATMEAL RAISIN COOKIES ❖

A healthy cookie with great flavor.

1/2 cup	butter OR margarine, softened	125 mL
1	egg	1
1/2 tsp.	vanilla	2 mL
3/4 cup	skim milk	175 mL
1 1/4 cups	unbleached all-purpose flour, sifted	300 mL
1/2 tsp.	baking powder	2 mL
3/4 cup	SPLENDA® Granular	175 mL
1 tsp.	cinnamon	5 mL
1 cup	rolled oats	250 mL
1/3 cup	raisins	75 mL

Cream butter. Add egg, vanilla and milk. Beat well. Combine flour, baking powder, SPLENDA® Granular and cinnamon. Stir in rolled oats and raisins. Combine the 2 mixtures and stir until moistened. Place level tablespoonfuls (15 mL) on greased cookie sheets. Flatten slightly with the back of a spoon. Bake in a 350°F (180°C) oven for 25-30 minutes, or until browned slightly. Cool on wire racks. **Yield: 20 large cookies.**

❖ COCONUT COOKIES ❖

Rich-tasting cookies with an attractive flaked coconut coating.

1 1/2 cups	all-purpose flour	375 mL
1 1/2 tsp.	baking powder	7 mL
1/4 tsp.	salt	1 mL
1 cup	SPLENDA® Granular	250 mL
1	egg, lightly beaten	1
1 tsp.	vanilla	5 mL
1 tsp.	coconut extract	5 mL
1/2 cup	butter OR margarine	125 mL
1/3 cup	medium, unsweetened coconut	75 mL
1 tbsp.	SPLENDA® Granular	15 mL

Sift the flour, baking powder and salt into a bowl. Stir in SPLENDA® Granular. Stir in the remaining ingredients, except the coconut. Take heaping teaspoons (5 mL) of dough and form into balls. Mix coconut and SPLENDA® Granular together. Press the dough balls into coconut, covering both sides and flatten into a round cookie shape. Place on a greased cookie sheet. Bake at 375°F (190°C) for 7-10 minutes. **Yield: 25 cookies.**

❖ JUMBO SPICE COOKIES ❖

This recipe was developed by my special friend, Maureen, who is a talented cookie baker. Thanks, Maureen.

1/2 cup	margarine OR butter, softened	125 mL
1 tsp.	vanilla	5 mL
1	egg	1
1	egg white	1
1 cup	SPLENDA® Granular	250 mL
1/2 cup	skim milk yogurt	125 mL
2 cups	all-purpose flour	500 mL
1 tsp.	baking soda	5 mL
1/2 tsp.	baking powder	2 mL
1/8 tsp.	ginger	0.5 mL
1/8 tsp.	nutmeg	0.5 mL
1 1/2 tsp.	cinnamon	7 mL
1/2-3/4 cup	raisins (optional)	125-175 mL

Preheat oven to 375°F (190°C). Beat the margarine, vanilla, eggs and SPLENDA® Granular together. Stir in the yogurt.

Sift dry ingredients together. Add liquid ingredients and stir to combine well. Fold in the raisins. Drop by 2 rounded tablespoons (30 mL), 1" (2.5 cm) apart onto an ungreased cookie sheet. Bake approximately 10 minutes, or until light brown. Cool slightly and remove from the cookie sheet. **Yield: 18 jumbo cookies or 36 smaller cookies.**

❖ TWIN COCONUT DROPS ❖

Pretty as a picture, chewy and not too sweet.

2	eggs	2
1/3 cup	all-purpose flour	75 mL
1/4 tsp.	baking powder	1 mL
1/8 tsp.	salt	0.5 mL
1 1/4 cups	SPLENDA® Granular	300 mL
1 tbsp.	diet margarine, melted	15 mL
1 tsp.	vanilla	5 mL
2 1/2 cups	unsweetened fine coconut	625 mL
1 oz.	unsweetened baking chocolate, melted	30 g
	a few red cherries, quartered, for garnish	

Continued.

Beat the eggs well.

Sift the flour, baking powder and salt together. Add SPLENDA®
Granular and stir well.

Fold the dry ingredients into the beaten eggs. With a fork stir in the
margarine, vanilla and coconut.

Divide the cookie batter in 2 portions. To half add the melted chocolate.
On a greased and floured cookie sheet, drop a teaspoon (5 mL) of each
batter next to each other, so that the 2 touch. Use a different spoon for
each batter. Garnish each cookie half with a small piece of cherry and
bake at 350°F (180°C) for 8-10 minutes, or until edges turn light brown.
Yield: approximately 20 cookies.

❖   BANANA CHOCOLATE   ❖
OAT SQUARES

A wonderfully healthy low-cal snack.

1/4 **cup**	**diet margarine**	**60 mL**
1/3 **cup**	**SPLENDA® Granular**	**75 mL**
1	**egg**	1
1 **tsp.**	**vanilla**	**5 mL**
1/4 **tsp.**	**salt**	**1 mL**
3	**bananas, mashed**	3
2 **cups**	**quick-cooking rolled oats**	**500 mL**
1 **oz.**	**semisweet baking chocolate (optional)**	**30 g**

Combine the margarine, SPLENDA® Granular, egg and vanilla. Beat
well. Add the salt and bananas. Beat again for 30 seconds. Stir in the
oats and scoop into a greased 8" (20 cm) square pan.

Bake at 350°F (180°C) for 25 minutes, or until firm and browning
slightly at the edges. Melt the chocolate and, using a knife, spread over
the banana oat mixture. Cool. **Yield: 9 squares.**

❖ CREAM CHEESE SWIRL BROWNIES ❖

Rich-tasting chocolate treats.

3 tbsp.	diet margarine	45 mL
2 tbsp.	cocoa	30 mL
3/4 cup	SPLENDA® Granular	175 mL
2 tbsp.	skim milk	30 mL
2 tbsp.	diet margarine	30 mL
3 oz.	light cream cheese, softened	85 g
1 cup	SPLENDA® Granular	250 mL
3	eggs	3
1/2 cup+1 tbsp.	all-purpose flour	140 mL
2 tsp.	vanilla	10 mL
1/2 tsp.	baking powder	2 mL
1/4 tsp.	salt	1 mL
1/4 tsp.	almond extract	1 mL

In a saucepan, melt the 3 tbsp. (45 mL) margarine. Stir in the cocoa, SPLENDA® Granular and skim milk. Set aside to cool.

Beat the 2 tbsp. (30 mL) of margarine with the softened cream cheese until smooth. Add 1/4 cup (60 mL) SPLENDA® Granular, 1 egg, 1 tbsp. (15 mL) flour and 1 tsp. (5 mL) vanilla. Blend. Set aside.

Beat 2 eggs very well and add the remaining 3/4 cup (190 mL) SPLENDA® Granular. Sift together the baking powder, salt and remaining 1/2 cup (125 mL) of flour and fold into the egg mixture. Stir in the cooled chocolate, the almond extract and remaining 1 tsp. (5 mL) vanilla. Set aside 1/3 cup (75 mL) of the chocolate batter.

Spread the remaining chocolate batter in a greased 8" (20 cm) square baking pan. Pour the cream cheese mixture evenly over the top. Drop the reserved chocolate batter by the teaspoonfuls (5 mL) on top and swirl with a knife. Bake at 350°F (180°C) for 15-20 minutes.
Yield: 16 brownies.

❖ PINEAPPLE COCONUT SQUARES ❖

If pineapple is your favorite fruit, then this is your square.

Crust:

1¹/4 cups	all-purpose flour	300 mL
¹/4 cup	SPLENDA® Granular	60 mL
¹/2 cup	margarine OR butter	125 mL

Filling:

19-oz.	can unsweetened crushed pineapple	540 mL
2 tbsp.	cornstarch	30 mL
³/4 cup	SPLENDA® Granular	175 mL
1 tbsp.	diet margarine	15 mL

Topping:

3	egg whites	3
¹/2 tsp.	cream of tartar	2 mL
¹/2 cup	SPLENDA® Granular	125 mL
1 cup	unsweetened fine coconut	250 mL

Crust: Stir the flour and SPLENDA® Granular together. Rub in the margarine and press down firmly into a 9 x 13" (23 x 33 cm) pan. Bake at 350°F (180°C) for 10 minutes. Cool.

Filling: In a saucepan, combine the crushed pineapple, cornstarch and SPLENDA® Granular; cook until the sauce is thickened and transparent. Remove from the heat and stir in the margarine. Allow to cool slightly and spread over the crust.

Topping: Beat the egg whites for 30 seconds on high, then add the cream of tartar and beat another 2 minutes, adding SPLENDA® Granular towards the end. Stir in coconut. Spread over the pineapple filling and bake at 350°F (180°C) for 15-20 minutes, or until browned slightly in places. Allow to cool thoroughly before cutting.

Yield: 24 squares.

❖ LEMON DELIGHT SQUARES ❖

Attractive and delicious squares.

Crust:

1/4 cup	diet margarine	60 mL
1 cup	graham cracker crumbs	250 mL
1/4 cup	SPLENDA® Granular	60 mL

Filling:

2/3 cup	all-purpose flour	150 mL
1 1/4 cups	SPLENDA® Granular	300 mL
2 tbsp.	water	30 mL
4	egg yolks	4
1/4 cup	commercially bottled lemon juice OR juice of 2 lemons	60 mL
2 tbsp.	finely grated lemon rind	30 mL
4	egg whites	4
1/2 tsp.	cream of tartar	2 mL
	sprinkle of graham cracker crumbs	

Crust: Melt the margarine and stir it into a mixture of the graham cracker crumbs and the first amount of SPLENDA® Granular. Press into an 8" (20 cm) square pan. Bake at 350°F (180°C) for 10 minutes. Set aside to cool.

Filling: In a heavy saucepan or double boiler, combine the flour, second amount of SPLENDA® Granular, water, egg yolks, lemon juice and grated lemon rind. With a wooden spoon, stir constantly over very low heat for about 5 minutes.

Beat the egg whites for 30 seconds until frothy, then add the cream of tartar and beat for a further 2 1/2 minutes. Fold the stiffly beaten egg whites into the lemon sauce and spread over the cooled crust. Sprinkle with graham cracker crumbs.

Bake at 350°F (180°C) for approximately 15 minutes. Switch off the oven and leave pan in for a further 5 minutes, or until squares are set. Allow to cool, loosen the edges and slice. **Yield: 16 squares.**

See photograph on the back cover.

❖ PUDDING ICING ❖

Creamy smooth.

1¹/₂ oz.	pkg. diet instant pudding mix (serves 4)	45 g
6 tbsp.	commercial low-calorie dessert topping mix (makes 3 cups [750 mL])	90 mL
²/₃ cup	SPLENDA® Granular	150 mL
1¹/₂ cups	cold skim milk	375 mL

Beat together all the ingredients until the icing has thickened. Try the various flavors, such as butterscotch, vanilla or chocolate.
Yield: Sufficient to fill and ice a 2-layer cake.

❖ For best results, make sure all the beating equipment is cold. Sometimes the amount of pudding mix is less than 1¹/₂ oz. (45 g). If the icing is too soft, beat in 1 tbsp. (15 mL) cornstarch.

❖ CHOCOLATE CREAM FROSTING ❖

Great chocolatey taste. Fill and frost the cake completely.

¹/₂ cup	commercial low-calorie dessert topping mix (makes 4 cups [1 L])	125 mL
1 tbsp.	cornstarch	15 mL
1 cup	cold skim milk	250 mL
³/₄ cup	SPLENDA® Granular	175 mL
¹/₄ cup	cocoa powder	60 mL
¹/₄ cup	skim milk yogurt	60 mL

Beat together all the ingredients, except the yogurt, until the frosting has thickened. Fold in the yogurt. Refrigerate for 30 minutes before frosting the cake.

Refrigerate the cake to preserve freshness. **Yield: Sufficient to fill and ice a 2-layer cake.**

❖ For best results, make sure all the beating equipment is cold.

❖ MOCHA CREAM FROSTING ❖

A wonderful coffee-flavored frosting.

1/2 cup	commercial low-calorie dessert topping mix (makes 4 cups [1 L])	125 mL
1 tbsp.	cornstarch	15 mL
3/4 cup	SPLENDA® Granular	175 mL
1 cup	cold skim milk	250 mL
1 1/2 tsp.	instant coffee	7 mL
1 tbsp.	hot water	15 mL

Beat together all the ingredients, except the coffee and water, until thickened. Add the instant coffee dissolved in hot water. Beat again until blended. If the frosting is too soft, beat in another 2 tsp. (10 mL) cornstarch. **Yield: Sufficient to fill and ice a 2-layer cake.**

❖ For best results, make sure all the beating equipment is cold.

See photograph on the back cover.

❖ ORANGE FROSTING ❖

A cream cheese icing high on taste and low in calories.

1 1/2 cups	2% cottage cheese	375 mL
4 oz.	light cream cheese	115 g
1 tbsp.	defrosted orange juice concentrate	15 mL
1 tsp.	orange extract	5 mL
3/4 cup	SPLENDA® Granular	175 mL
1 tbsp.	finely grated orange rind (optional)	15 mL

In a food processor or blender with a sharp blade, process the cottage cheese until smooth. Add the rest of the ingredients except the orange rind. Beat until smooth. Add the grated orange rind and beat until evenly distributed throughout the frosting. **Yield: Sufficient to fill and ice a 2-layer cake.**

❖ WONDERFUL CREAMY ❖
CUSTARD SAUCE

Great over fresh fruit or jelly desserts.

1/4 cup	skim milk	60 mL
3 tbsp.	custard powder	45 mL
2 tbsp.	skim milk	30 mL
2	egg yolks	2
2 1/4 cups	skim milk	550 mL
1/3 cup+1 tbsp.	SPLENDA® Granular	90 mL
1 tsp.	vanilla	5 mL

Gradually add the first amount of milk to the custard powder, stirring until smooth. Set aside. Using a fork, lightly mix the 2 tbsp. (30 mL) milk with the egg yolks. Set aside.

Bring the 2 1/4 cups (550 mL) skim milk to a boil. Stir in the custard mixture and SPLENDA® Granular. Cook until thickened. Stir some of the hot milk mixture into the egg yolk mixture and return to the saucepan. Stir over low heat until the egg is cooked (do not boil) and the sauce is slightly thickened. Cool a little and add the vanilla. Cover the surface with plastic wrap to prevent a skin from forming. Refrigerate. **Yield: 3 cups (750 mL).**

❖ After several hours of refrigeration, the Custard Sauce may be less creamy in consistency. If this happens, place in a blender and blend until smooth.

❖ STRAWBERRY SAUCE ❖

Great over crêpes, waffles, pancakes or vanilla ice cream.

2 cups	fresh OR frozen, unsweetened, thawed, drained strawberries	500 mL
1/4 cup	reserved strawberry juice from thawing OR water	60 mL
2 tsp.	cornstarch	10 mL
1/4 cup	SPLENDA® Granular	60 mL

If using frozen strawberries, allow to thaw at room temperature until completely defrosted. If desired, the strawberries may be cut in half before cooking.

In a saucepan, gradually add the reserved juice or water to the cornstarch, stirring until smooth. Add strawberries and SPLENDA® Granular. Stir over medium heat until sauce thickens and is translucent. **Yield: 2 cups (500 mL) sauce.**

VARIATIONS: Strawberry Apple Sauce — Replace the strawberry juice or water with an equal amount of apple juice. Remove from heat when the sauce is thickened and translucent. Stir in 1 tsp. (5 mL) lemon juice.

Raspberry or Peach Sauce — Replace strawberries and liquid with equal amounts of raspberries and liquid or peaches and liquid. You may have to add additional SPLENDA® Granular if the fruit is tart.

❖ BLUEBERRY SAUCE ❖

Any frozen berry can be substituted in this versatile sauce.

1/2 cup	orange juice	125 mL
1/4 cup	SPLENDA® Granular	60 mL
2 tbsp.	cornstarch	30 mL
2 cups	frozen, unsweetened blueberries	500 mL

In a saucepan, combine the juice, SPLENDA® Granular and cornstarch. Whisk until the cornstarch dissolves. Add the blueberries. Cook over medium heat, stirring until the sauce is thick and translucent. Yield: 2 cups (500 mL).

❖ APPLESAUCE ❖

What a wonderful aroma. Useful in many recipes.

3 lbs.	cooking apples, peeled and sliced	1.5 kg
3/4 cup	boiling water	175 mL
1/4 tsp.	ground cinnamon	1 mL
8	cloves	8
3/4 cup	SPLENDA® Granular	175 mL

In a large saucepan, combine all the ingredients, except SPLENDA® Granular, and heat to boiling. Reduce the heat to medium low. Cover and simmer, stirring occasionally. Cook 20 minutes for chunky applesauce and 30 minutes for smooth applesauce (mash lightly, if necessary). Stir occasionally.

In the last minutes before the end of cooking time, add SPLENDA® Granular and stir well. Remove the cloves. **Yield: 3 cups (750 mL).**

❖ STRAWBERRY JAM ❖

You can really taste the fruit in this jam.

6 cups	frozen, unsweetened, thawed strawberries (fresh, sliced strawberries may be substituted in season)	1.5 L
1/2 tsp.	butter	2 mL
2 1/2-3 cups	SPLENDA® Granular (to taste)	625-750 mL
1 3/4 oz.	pkg. light OR sugarless pectin	49 g
1 tbsp.	unflavored gelatin (1 env.)	15 mL
1 tbsp.	cold water	15 mL

Crush the strawberries and place in a large, heavy enamel or stainless steel saucepan. Add the butter to prevent too much foaming. Combine 1/4 cup (60 mL) of the measured amount of SPLENDA® Granular with the pectin. Stir into the fruit and bring to a full boil over high heat, stirring constantly.

Add remaining SPLENDA® Granular and boil a couple of minutes, stirring constantly. Remove from the heat and skim the foam off the surface of the jam. Return the saucepan to the heat and stir in the envelope of unflavored gelatin, soaked in 1 tbsp. (15 mL) cold water. Stir until it dissolves. Remove the saucepan from the heat.

Pour the jam into sterilized jars, leaving a 1/8" (3 mm) space, seal and boil in a water bath canner, covering the jars with at least 1" (2.5 cm) of water, for 10 minutes. Place the lid on the water bath canner and time from the moment the water boils. Remove. The disc will snap down after the jam has cooled. This recipe makes enough jam to fill 2, 16 oz. (500 mL) jam jars. If desired, smaller jam jars may be used. Refrigerate. The jam will thicken over the next day. Freeze the jam no more than 1 year. If freezing, leave a 1/2" (1.3 cm) of head space to allow for expansion.

After opening, the jam will last a few weeks in the refrigerator.
Yield: 4 cups (1 L).

VARIATIONS: Make your favorite fruit jams. Substitute sliced peaches or apricots (add 2 tbsp. [30 mL] lemon juice), plums or cherries or whole raspberries or blueberries, etc., for strawberries.

❖ Generally the rule of thumb is a 2:1 ratio, use twice as much fruit as SPLENDA® Granular.

❖ INDEX ❖

86

Share *SPLENDID DESSERTS* with a friend

Order **SPLENDID DESSERTS** at $9.95 per book plus $3.00 (total order) for shipping and handling.

Number of books _____ x $9.95 = $ _____
Postage and handling _____ = $ ____3.00
Subtotal _____ = $ _____
In Canada add 7% GST _____ (Subtotal x .07) = $ _____
Total enclosed _____ = $ _____

U.S. and international orders payable in U.S. funds./ Price is subject to change.

NAME: _____
STREET:_____
CITY: _____ PROV./STATE _____
COUNTRY _____ POSTAL CODE/ZIP _____

Please make cheque or money order payable to:　　**Eureka Publishing
P.O. Box 2305
Station "M"
CALGARY, Alberta
Canada T2P 2M6**

For fund raising or volume purchases, contact **EUREKA PUBLISHING** for volume rates.
Please allow 2-3 weeks for delivery.

❖　　**Buy 5 books — get the 6th book free**　❖

Share *SPLENDID DESSERTS* with a friend

Order **SPLENDID DESSERTS** at $9.95 per book plus $3.00 (total order) for shipping and handling.

Number of books _____ x $9.95 = $ _____
Postage and handling _____ = $ ____3.00
Subtotal _____ = $ _____
In Canada add 7% GST _____ (Subtotal x .07) = $ _____
Total enclosed _____ = $ _____

U.S. and international orders payable in U.S. funds./ Price is subject to change.

NAME: _____
STREET:_____
CITY: _____ PROV./STATE _____
COUNTRY _____ POSTAL CODE/ZIP _____

Please make cheque or money order payable to:　　**Eureka Publishing
P.O. Box 2305
Station "M"
CALGARY, Alberta
Canada T2P 2M6**

For fund raising or volume purchases, contact **EUREKA PUBLISHING** for volume rates.
Please allow 2-3 weeks for delivery.

❖　　**Buy 5 books — get the 6th book free**　❖

❖ AUTHOR'S NOTE ❖

We are in the twentieth century and now it seems the impossible is true. We can have our cake and eat it too!!! Sugarless, low-fat, low-calorie desserts that taste every bit like the real thing are here to stay, thanks to a major breakthrough in the low-calorie sweetener market.

SPLENDA® LOW-CALORIE SWEETENER is the only low-calorie sweetener created from sugar. This chemically inert sugar substitute tastes like sugar and is suitable for cooking and baking because of its incredible heat stability. It has been rigorously tested over 17 years and has been proven to be safe as it does not accumulate in the body. In addition, studies show that sucralose (the common name) has no effect on blood glucose, blood fructose and/or insulin secretion in both people with and without diabetes.

My interest in this sugar substitute grew out of a need in our family. My husband could no longer tolerate sugar. I love to bake and was sure we would all feel deprived, but then SPLENDA® Granular came to the rescue! Happily, it does not affect moods or promote tooth decay either. Upon experimenting, I realized that a cookbook was necessary, as it was not always a matter of simple substitution. SPLENDA® Granular has very little density (weighing ⅛ as much as sugar) and therefore imparts less structure and volume to baked products. This cookbook is a comprehensive guide for baking with SPLENDA® Granular and soon you will develop an intuitive feel for baking with this amazing product. Please remember to keep an eye open for Volume 2 of *Splendid Desserts* in the second half of 1995!

SPLENDA® LOW-CALORIE SWEETENER is the registered trademark of McNeil Consumer Products Company. McNeil Consumer Products Company has not been involved in the production or distribution of this cookbook.

Although I have totally satisfied myself of the safety of SPLENDA® Granular, it is up to each individual to decide that independently. For more information on the safety of SPLENDA® LOW-CALORIE SWEETENER call 1-800-561-0070 in Canada or write to SPLENDA® Information Center,P.O. Box 1390, Guelph, Ontario, Canada N1K 1A5, OR write to SPLENDA® Information Center, P.O. Box 1268, New Brunswick, NJ, USA 08903-1268.